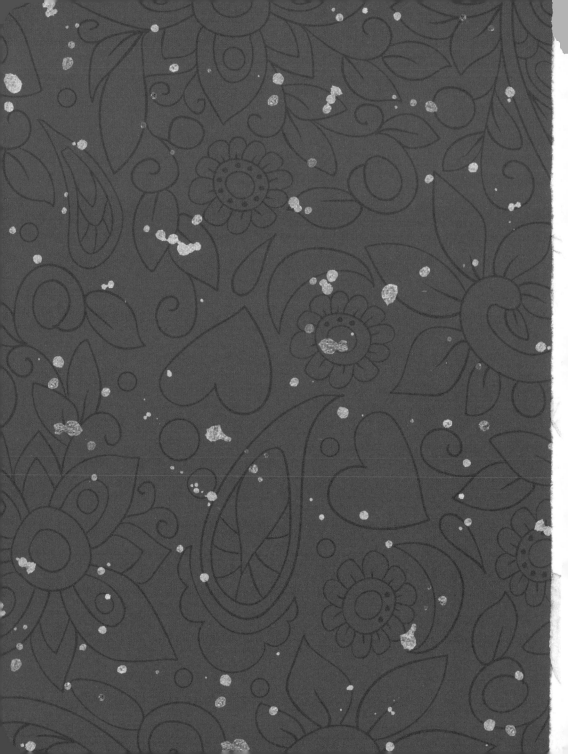

100 DEVOTIONS

for coloring & creative journaling

Inspire®

Faith, Hope & Love

Tyndale House Publishers
Carol Stream, Illinois

Visit Tyndale online at Tyndale.com.

Tyndale, Tyndale's quill logo, *New Living Translation, NLT,* and *Inspire* are registered trademarks of Tyndale House Ministries.

Inspire: Faith, Hope & Love copyright © 2023 by Tyndale House Publishers. All rights reserved.

Reflections on Faith copyright © 2010, 2023 by Tyndale House Publishers. All rights reserved.

Reflections on Hope copyright © 2010, 2023 by Tyndale House Publishers. All rights reserved.

Reflections on Love copyright © 2010, 2023 by Tyndale House Publishers. All rights reserved.

Compiled and Edited by Mark R. Norton

Interior design and typesetting by Peachtree Publishing Services

Cover design by Nicole Grimes

Scripture quotations are taken from the *Holy Bible,* New Living Translation, copyright © 1996, 2004, 2015 by Tyndale House Foundation. Used by permission of Tyndale House Publishers, Carol Stream, Illinois 60188. All rights reserved.

ISBN 978-1-4964-7197-0

Printed in China

29 28 27 26 25 24 23
7 6 5 4 3 2 1

Contents

THREE THINGS
WILL LAST FOREVER—
faith, hope,
and love.
1 CORINTHIANS 13:13

Preface

*"Three things will last forever—faith, hope, and love—
and the greatest of these is love."*

1 Corinthians 13:13

We live in a world in constant motion and never-ending change. We sometimes find ourselves almost desperate to escape. Nothing seems stable. Where can we find a solid foundation to stand on?

Stop a moment. Listen. God is always present. And God is always speaking. Through His Word, God offers a constant flow of life-giving words—words of faith, hope, and love. These foundation stones are forever. They call us away from the madness and point to the God who never changes. He is the reliable focus of our faith, the eternal reason for our hope, and the unstoppable source of faithful love.

You are opening the door to a sacred space. Relax, reflect, and connect to God through creative expression. Let this beautifully designed collection of reflections on faith, hope, and love awaken these life-changing attributes in your own heart and life. Let each devotional encourage you to stand strongly in your faith, lean firmly on God's hope, and rest deeply in God's love. As you actively worship through this book, look forward to the day when all believers—past, present, and future—will join in one great chorus around God's throne. And remember that even there, faith, hope, and love will still remain. Through these reflections, we can begin to grasp some of the realities of heaven.

Made Righteous by Faith

And Abram believed the LORD,
and the LORD counted him as
righteous because of his faith.

(Genesis 15:6)

Abram had demonstrated his faith through his actions by leaving his homeland at God's request even when it didn't make much sense in human terms. But it was Abram's belief in the Lord, not his actions, that established his relationship with God and made him right in God's sight (Romans 4:1-5). We, too, can have a right relationship with God by trusting Him and His promises to us.

Our outward actions—things like church attendance, prayer, and acts of service—will not themselves make us right with God. A right relationship with God always depends on faith—the heartfelt confidence that God is who He says He is and does what He says He will do. Right actions will follow naturally as by-products of our faith. Once we truly believe God and understand His love for us, our natural response should be to love and obey Him.

Insights:

....

....

....

....

....

....

....

The Lord
counted him
AS RIGHTEOUS
BECAUSE OF HIS FAITH.
Genesis 15:6

God's Unfailing Love

The LORD passed in front of Moses, calling out, "Yahweh! The LORD! The
God of compassion and mercy! I am slow to anger and filled with unfail-
ing love and faithfulness. I lavish unfailing love to a thousand generations.
I forgive iniquity, rebellion, and sin. But I do not excuse the guilty."

(Exodus 34:6-7)

Moses had asked to see God's glorious presence (see Exodus 33:18), and this was God's response. How did God define His glory? It is His character, His nature, His way of relating to His creation. And notice that God gave Moses a vision not of His power but of His love. God's glory is revealed in His mercy, grace, compassion, faithfulness, forgiveness, and justice. God's love and mercy are truly wonderful, and we benefit from them in all these ways.

Many people think the God of the Old Testament is a God of wrath, only to be feared, but these words from God revealed to Moses the very heart of God's nature. What do we learn from these assurances to Moses? God is, at His very core, compassionate, merciful, loving, faithful, and forgiving. Don't accept anyone's argument that the God of the Old Testament is merely vengeful. Instead, remember that God is slow to anger and His love can never be diminished.

Insights:

....

....

....

....

....

....

....

"I AM SLOW TO ANGER AND FILLED WITH UNFAILING LOVE AND FAITHFULNESS."

EXODUS 34:6

Love Leads to Obedience

You must love the LORD your God with all your heart, all
your soul, and all your strength. And you must commit yourselves wholeheartedly to these commands that I am giving
you today. Repeat them again and again to your children.

(Deuteronomy 6:5-7)

Jesus said that loving God with our entire self—heart, soul, mind,
and strength—is the first and greatest commandment (Matthew
22:37-40). This command, combined with the command to love our
neighbor (Leviticus 19:18), encompasses all the other Old Testament
laws. So when God asks us to commit ourselves wholeheartedly to
His commands, this is simply an extension of His command that we
love Him wholeheartedly. If we love God, we will seek to obey Him.

If you are a parent, the key to teaching your children to love God
is stated simply and clearly in these verses: If you want your children to follow God, you must make Him a part of your everyday
experiences. You must show your children that God is active in all
aspects of life, not just the things that happen at church. Loving God
includes bringing Him home.

Insights:

....

....

....

....

....

....

....

....

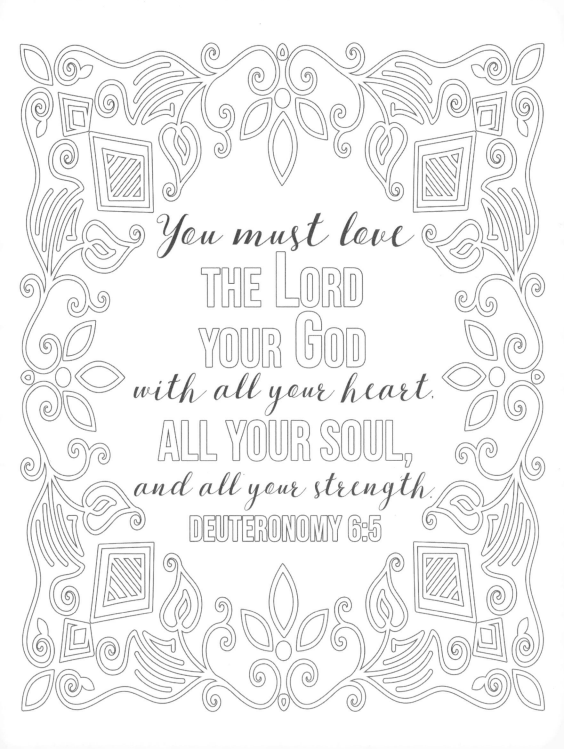

Faith Overcomes Fear

"Don't be afraid!" Elisha told him. "For there are more on our side than on theirs!" Then Elisha prayed, "O LORD, open his eyes and let him see!" The LORD opened the young man's eyes, and when he looked up, he saw that the hillside around Elisha was filled with horses and chariots of fire.

(2 Kings 6:16-17)

Elisha's servant was no longer afraid when he saw God's mighty heavenly army all around. Faith reveals that God is doing more for His people than we can ever realize through our sight alone. Our faith in God in itself becomes evidence in our hearts that God is present and that His power and protection are truly available to us.

When we face difficulties that seem insurmountable, we must remember that spiritual resources are present even if we cannot see them. We need to learn to see with eyes of faith, allowing God to reveal His resources to us. When we cannot see God working in our lives, the problem could be our spiritual eyesight, not a lack of God's presence or power. Ask God to open your eyes so you can truly see!

Insights:

....

....

....

....

....

....

....

We need
TO LEARN TO SEE
with eyes of faith.

God's Loving Protection

Show me your unfailing love in wonderful ways. By
your mighty power you rescue those who seek refuge
from their enemies. Guard me as you would guard your
own eyes. Hide me in the shadow of your wings.

(Psalm 17:7-8)

Our circumstances may cause us to question whether God is present in our lives. Like the psalm writer, we can ask God to show His love to us. If life seems bleak and overwhelming, ask God to remind you of His love for you today. His reminder may come from a friend, a song you hear, the beauty of God's creation, or a Bible verse He brings to your mind. When you notice it, recognize it as a way God has chosen to communicate with you, and thank Him for this sign of His love.

The psalmist uses a few illustrations here for God's loving protection. Just as we reflexively shield our eyes, God will always protect us. And He guards us just as a mother bird protects her young by sheltering them in the shadow of her wings. We must not conclude, however, that we have some-how missed God's protection if we experience troubles. God's protection has far greater purposes than helping us avoid pain; it is to make us better servants for Him. One way God protects us is by guiding us through painful circumstances, not only by helping us escape them.

Insights:

....

....

....

....

....

....

....

God's Love for All Creation

Your unfailing love, O LORD, is as vast as the heavens; your
faithfulness reaches beyond the clouds. Your righteousness is like the mighty mountains, your justice like the ocean
depths. You care for people and animals alike, O LORD.

(Psalm 36:5-6)

In contrast to the wicked and their evil plots that end in failure, God will always triumph. He is faithful, righteous, and just. His love is as vast as the heavens; His faithfulness reaches beyond the clouds; His righteousness is as solid as the mountains; His judgments are as full of wisdom as the oceans are with water. We need not fear evil people because we know that God loves us, judges evil, and will care for us throughout eternity.

The psalmist praises God for His tender care of all living creatures, not just people. Although humans are made uniquely in God's image and hold a special leadership role in creation, it is clear that God also has deep affection for His other creatures, which are all part of His marvelous creation. From the very beginning God showed His love for the animals. He even assigned Adam to give them all names (Genesis 2:18-20). And though we don't elevate animals to the same status as human beings, God's created order calls us to care for them and our world, just as God's representatives should.

Insights:

....

....

....

....

....

....

....

Hope in God Alone

We are merely moving shadows, and all our busy
rushing ends in nothing. We heap up wealth, not
knowing who will spend it. And so, Lord, where
do I put my hope? My only hope is in you.

(Psalm 39:6-7)

Life is short no matter how long we live. If we have something important we want to do, we must not put it off for a better day. Ask yourself,
*If I had only six months to live, what would I do? Tell some important
people how I really feel about them? Deal with an undisciplined area of
my life? Tell someone about Jesus?* Because life is short, we cannot neglect
what is truly important.

The brevity of life is a theme found often in Scripture. Ironically,
most people spend much time trying to secure their lives on earth but
give little thought to where they will spend eternity. The psalmist realized that busily amassing riches would make no difference in eternity.
Few people understand that their only real hope is in the Lord. The
answer to the question of meaning in life cannot be found in this world
or made up ourselves. It can only be found in God.

Insights:

....

....

....

....

....

....

....

Faith Like a Child

How kind the Lord is! How good he is! So merciful,
this God of ours! The Lord protects those of childlike
faith; I was facing death, and he saved me. Let my soul
be at rest again, for the Lord has been good to me.

(Psalm 116:5-7)

God loves to respond to us, so He is always available when we reach out to Him. He bends down and listens to our voice. He gets down on our level and looks into our eyes. Even though He has millions of children, He can focus fully on each one of us. The psalm writer's faith in the Lord had grown because he had experienced answers to his prayers. If you are discouraged, remember that God our Father is near, listening carefully to every prayer and answering each one in His timing to give you His best.

God stays close to us even when we are facing death. When a believer we love is nearing death, we will be filled with sorrow, but we can find comfort by remembering that those who believe in God are precious to God (Psalm 116:15) and that He has carefully chosen the time when they will be called into His presence. God sees, and each life is valuable to Him.

Insights:

....

....

....

....

....

....

....

The LORD protects those of childlike faith.

Psalm 116:6

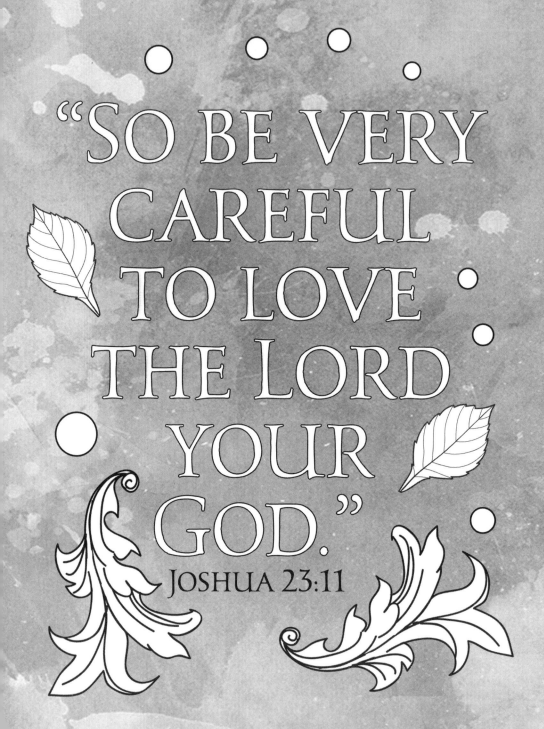

Worthy of Our Hope

I look up to the mountains—does my help
come from there? My help comes from
the LORD, who made heaven and earth!

(Psalm 121:1-2)

This psalm expresses assurance and hope in God's eternal protection, day and night. The psalm writer asks if his help comes from the mountains. The answer to this question is no. It was on the mountains that pagan peoples offered sacrifices at their high places to their false gods. So where do we look for help? We look to the Lord, the Creator of the mountains and hills, and of all heaven and earth as well.

We should never trust a lesser power than God Himself or believe that answers to life's deepest questions can be found in nature or this world's wisdom. Not only is God all-powerful, but He also watches over us. He watches us like a sentinel or shepherd, alert to danger and ready to help with our needs. Nothing diverts or deters Him. We are safe. Let us welcome God's caring and untiring watch over our lives.

Insights:

....

....

....

....

....

....

....

....

Hope in God's Strength

Those who trust in the LORD will find new strength.
They will soar high on wings like eagles. They will run
and not grow weary. They will walk and not faint.

(Isaiah 40:31)

Even the strongest people get tired at times, but God's power and strength never diminish. He is never too tired or too busy to help or listen. His strength is our source of strength and hope. When you feel life crushing you and you cannot go another step, remember that you can call upon God to renew your strength and help you find new hope.

Part of trusting in the Lord is expecting that His promise of strength will help us rise above life's difficulties. Like eagles, we need to discover that soaring high is more dependent on the force of rising air currents than on wing strength. And God's Spirit is always moving beneath our wings. Do you believe that God loves you and wants the best for you? Can you relax, confident that His purposes are right? Are you convinced that He has the power to control all of life—and your own life as well?

Insights:

....

....

....

....

....

....

....

....

Faith, Even under Fire

"God blesses you when people mock you and persecute you and lie about
you and say all sorts of evil things against you because you are my followers.
Be happy about it! Be very glad! For a great reward awaits you in heaven.
And remember, the ancient prophets were persecuted in the same way."

(Matthew 5:11-12)

Jesus expects us to experience persecution for our faith, and He told us to be
happy when that happens. Jesus' first disciples were persecuted by hostile authorities, who were offended by Jesus' teaching and threatened by their own loss of
power over people's lives. Ever since, associating with Jesus and obeying His teach-
ings have often been a source of persecution.

So how can we be happy about persecution when it happens? One way is to
understand how persecution can be good: (1) it takes our eyes off earthly rewards,
(2) it strips away superficial belief, (3) it strengthens the faith of those who endure,
and (4) our attitude through it serves as an example for others to follow. We can
also be comforted knowing that God's greatest prophets were persecuted (Elijah,
Jeremiah, Daniel, John). But most of all, when we are faithful to Jesus, no matter
what the cost might be, we can be sure that a great reward awaits us in heaven.
God will reward the faithful by receiving them into His eternal Kingdom, where
there is no more persecution.

Insights:

....

....

....

....

....

....

....

Loving as God Loves

"You have heard the law that says, 'Love your neighbor' and hate your enemy. But I say, love your enemies! Pray for those who persecute you!"

(Matthew 5:43-44)

When we are wronged, often our first reaction is to get even. Instead, Jesus said we should do good to those who wrong us! Our desire should be not to keep score but to love and forgive. This is not natural—it is supernatural. Only God can give us the strength to love the way He does. Instead of planning vengeance, pray for those who hurt you. By telling us not to retaliate, Jesus keeps us from taking the law into our own hands. By loving and praying for our enemies, we can overcome evil with good.

These verses from Matthew contain a reference to Old Testament passages. The Pharisees interpreted Leviticus 19:18 as teaching that they should love only those who love in return, and Psalms 139:19-22 and 140:9-11 as meaning that they should hate their enemies. But Jesus says we are to love our enemies. If you love your enemies and treat them well, you will truly show that Jesus is Lord of your life. This is possible only for those who give themselves fully to God, because only He can deliver people from natural selfishness.

Insights:

....

....

....

....

....

....

....

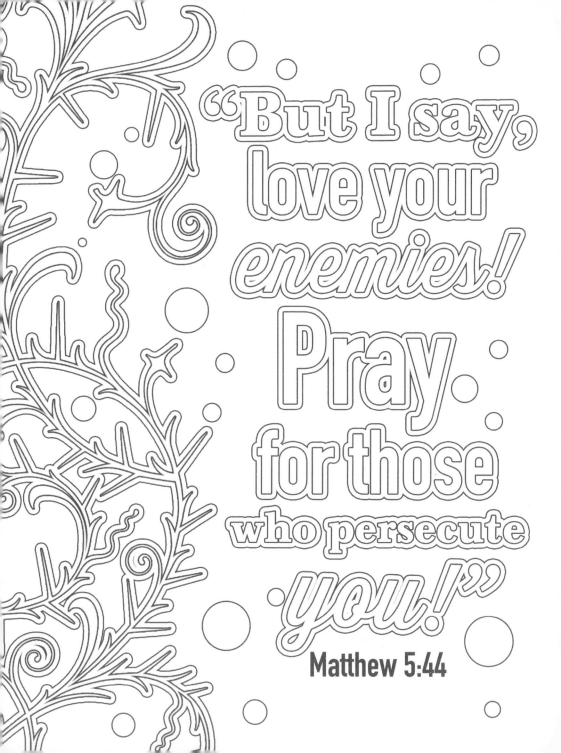

"But I say, love your enemies! Pray for those who persecute you!"

Matthew 5:44

Faith in the Right Things

"Don't store up treasures here on earth, where moths eat them and rust destroys
them, and where thieves break in and steal. Store your treasures in heaven,
where moths and rust cannot destroy, and thieves do not break in and steal.
Wherever your treasure is, there the desires of your heart will also be."

(Matthew 6:19-21)

Storing treasures in heaven is not limited to giving our money to God;
it is accomplished by all acts of faithful obedience to Him. There is a
sense in which giving our time and money to God's work is like invest-
ing in heaven. Our fearless giving certainly demonstrates our faith in
God's promises—that He can take care of us better than our money
can. Faith in God is the only firm foundation on which to build a life.

Jesus made it clear that placing our faith in the wrong "treasures"
leads our hearts to the wrong place. What we put our faith in controls
us, whether we admit it or not. If possessions or money become too
important to us, we must reestablish control or get rid of items. Jesus
calls for a decision that allows us to live contentedly with whatever we
have because we have chosen to trust in Him instead of the false security that our temporary, earthly treasures might seem to offer.

Insights:

....

....

....

....

....

....

....

....

Ultimate Allegiance

"No one can serve two masters. For you will hate one and
love the other; you will be devoted to one and despise the
other. You cannot serve God and be enslaved to money."

(Matthew 6:24)

Jesus contrasted heavenly values with earthly values when He explained that our first
love should be for things that do not fade, cannot be stolen or used up, and never wear
out. We should not be fascinated with our possessions, lest they possess us. God alone
deserves our love. Either we store our treasures with God (Matthew 6:20-21), focus
our eyes on Him (Matthew 6:22-23), and serve Him alone—or else we do not serve
Him at all. Where does your ultimate allegiance lie?

Jesus says we can have only one master. We live in a materialistic society in which
many people serve money. They spend all their lives collecting and storing it, only to
die and leave it behind. Their desire for money and what it can buy far outweighs their
commitment to God and spiritual matters. Whatever you store up, you will spend
much of your time and energy thinking about it. Don't fall into the materialistic trap,
because "the love of money is the root of all kinds of evil" (1 Timothy 6:10). Can
you honestly say that God, and not money, is your master? One test is to ask yourself
which one occupies more of your thoughts, time, and efforts.

Insights:

....

....

....

....

....

....

....

Genuine Faith Required

"Not everyone who calls out to me, 'Lord! Lord!' will enter the Kingdom of Heaven. Only those who actually do the will of my Father in heaven will enter. On judgment day many will say to me, 'Lord! Lord! We prophesied in your name and cast out demons in your name and performed many miracles in your name.' But I will reply, 'I never knew you.'"

(Matthew 7:21-23)

Jesus exposes those who sound religious but have no personal relationship with Him. It is tempting to think that one's accomplishments carry weight with God—especially if those accomplishments have the flavor of religion. We tend to think that feeding the poor, helping those who are suffering in some fashion, or doing other good deeds will make us "right" with God. Those are all good things, but as good as they are, they are not the same as having a living relationship with God through Jesus Christ.

On "judgment day" only our relationship with Christ—our acceptance of Him as Savior and our obedience to Him—will count. Many people think that if they are "good" people and say religious things, they will be rewarded with eternal life. In reality, faith in Christ is what will count at the judgment. A genuine relationship with Him demonstrated by a life lived in His service is the only pathway to eternal life.

Insights:
....
....
....
....
....
....
....

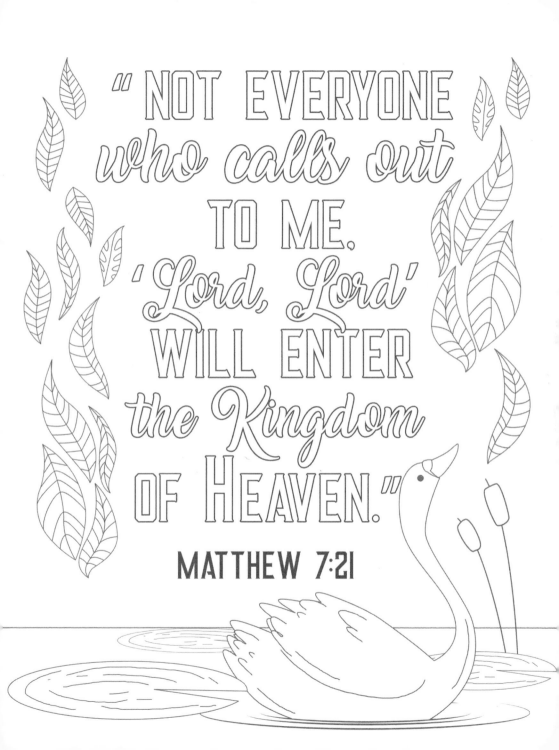

"NOT EVERYONE who calls out TO ME, 'Lord, Lord' WILL ENTER the Kingdom OF HEAVEN."

MATTHEW 7:21

Reaching Out to Touch Christ

Just then a woman who had suffered for twelve years with constant bleeding came up behind him. She touched the fringe of his robe, for she thought, "If I can just touch his robe, I will be healed." Jesus turned around, and when he saw her he said, "Daughter, be encouraged! Your faith has made you well." And the woman was healed at that moment.

(Matthew 9:20-22)

It was virtually impossible to get close to Jesus, but one woman fought her way desperately through the crowd in order to touch Him. She had been afflicted by physical infirmity for many years, and she wanted healing. She believed that touching Jesus would bring the healing she longed for. As soon as she did, she was healed. What a difference between the crowds who are curious about Jesus and the few who reach out and touch Him!

Today, many people are vaguely familiar with Jesus, but nothing in their lives is changed or bettered by this passing acquaintance. Only faith reaches out to touch Christ. Only faith in Christ releases God's healing power. Are you just curious about God, or do you reach out to Him in faith, knowing that His mercy will bring healing to your body, soul, and spirit? Move beyond curiosity. Reach out to Christ in faith. That touch will change your life forever.

Insights:

....

....

....

....

....

....

....

....

Give thanks TO THE LORD, FOR HE IS GOOD! His faithful love ENDURES FOREVER.

1 CHRONICLES 16:34

Determined Faith

After Jesus left the girl's home, two blind
men followed along behind him, shouting, "Son of David, have mercy on us!"

(Matthew 9:27)

The blind men needed God's mercy, and they knew Jesus could give it to them. They lived in a society where those who were blind remained destitute and helpless, and where their blindness was viewed as a judgment from God (see John 9:2). They needed God's help, and they knew that the Messiah, the Son of David, would give sight to the blind (Isaiah 29:18-19; 35:5-6). They recognized Jesus as that Messiah, so they followed Him, pleading for mercy.

Jesus didn't respond immediately to the blind men's pleas. He waited to see if they had faith. Not everyone who needs help really believes God can help. Then, when Jesus questioned these men, He drew out of them an affirmation of their faith in Jesus. When you think that God is too slow in answering your prayers, consider that He might be testing you as He did the blind men. Do you believe that God can help you? Do you really want His help? Be ready to affirm your faith as you wait on Him to help you.

Insights:

....

....

....

....

....

....

....

Be ready
to affirm
your faith
as you wait
on Him
to help you.

Valued in God's Eyes

"What is the price of two sparrows—one copper coin? But not a single sparrow can fall to the ground without your Father knowing it. And the very hairs on your head are all numbered. So don't be afraid; you are more valuable to God than a whole flock of sparrows."

(Matthew 10:29-31)

Jesus said that God is aware of everything that happens, even to sparrows, and you are far more valuable to Him than they are. You are so valuable that God sent His only Son to die for you (John 3:16). Because God places such value on you, you need never fear personal threats or difficult trials. These can't shake God's love or dislodge His Spirit from within you. A situation is never hopeless when God is there.

This doesn't mean, however, that God will take away all your troubles (see Matthew 10:16). The real test of value is how well something holds up under the wear, tear, and stress of everyday life. Those who stand up for Christ in spite of their troubles truly have lasting value and will receive great rewards (see Matthew 5:11-12).

Insights:

....

....

....

....

....

....

....

....

Loving the Least of These

"Anyone who receives you receives me, and anyone who receives me receives the Father who sent me. . . . If you give even a cup of cold water to one of the least of my followers, you will surely be rewarded."

(Matthew 10:40-42)

How much we love God can be measured by how well we treat others. Jesus' example of giving a cup of cold water to one of the least of His followers is a good model for unselfish service. Such a person usually can't or won't return a favor. God notices the good deeds we do as though He were the one receiving them. Is there something unselfish you can do for someone else today? God will notice, even if no one else does.

And remember that real love is an action, not a feeling. The greatest act of love is to give up your life for another person. How can this be done? By serving others with no thought of receiving anything in return. Sometimes it is easier to say we'll die for others than to live for them selflessly—this involves putting the desires of others before our own.

Insights:

....

....

....

....

....

....

....

....

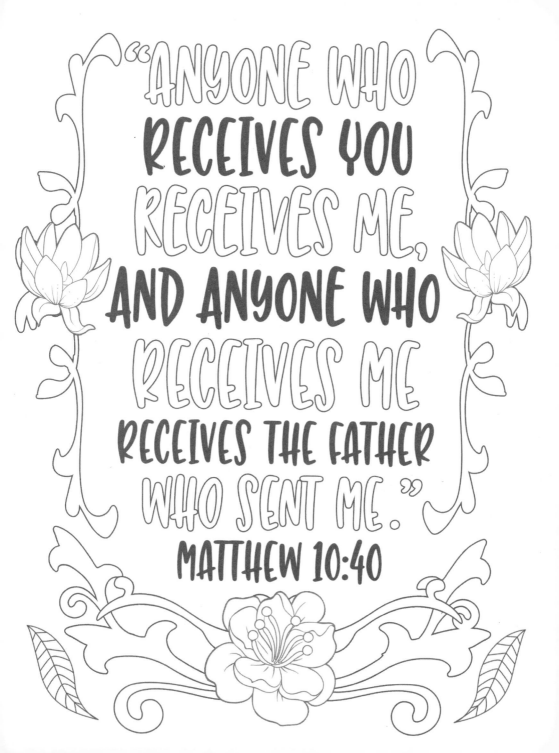

Good Intentions, Faltering Faith

But when [Peter] saw the strong wind and the waves, he was
terrified and began to sink. "Save me, Lord!" he shouted.
Jesus immediately reached out and grabbed him. "You have
so little faith," Jesus said. "Why did you doubt me?"

(Matthew 14:30-31)

Peter started out with good intentions. When he saw Jesus walking
toward the disciples on the water, Peter thought that he could, too, if
Jesus told him to. Peter believed that Jesus had the power to hold him
up. Peter was right, and Jesus' power sustained him as he began to
walk on the water. But when Peter looked at the stormy sea, his faith
faltered, and he began to sink.

Although we start out with good intentions, sometimes our faith
falters. This doesn't necessarily mean we have failed. When Peter's
faith faltered, he reached out to Christ, the only one who could help.
He was afraid, but he still looked to Christ. When you are apprehen-
sive about the troubles around you and doubt Christ's presence or
ability to help, remember that He is always with you and is the only
one who can really help. Reach out to Him, and experience the help
that He gives to those who trust in Him.

Insights:
....

....

....

....

....

....

....

....

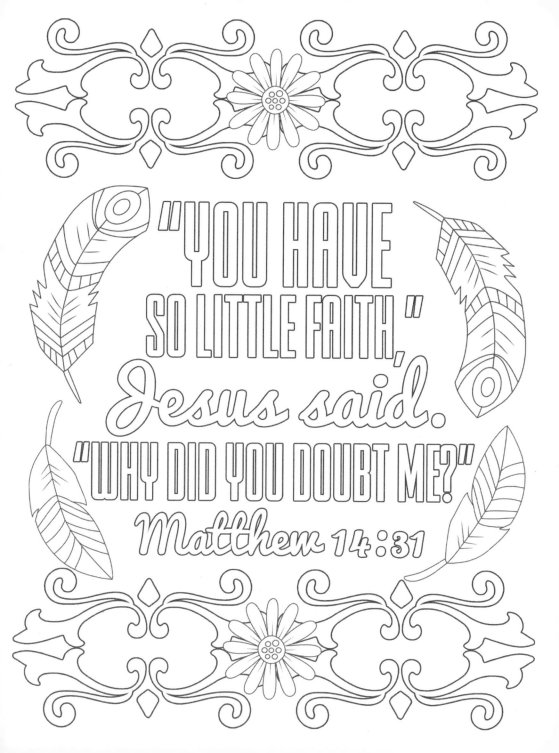

"YOU HAVE SO LITTLE FAITH," Jesus said. "WHY DID YOU DOUBT ME?" Matthew 14:31

The Tiniest Faith

"You don't have enough faith," Jesus told them. "I tell you
the truth, if you had faith even as small as a mustard seed,
you could say to this mountain, 'Move from here to there,'
and it would move. Nothing would be impossible."

(Matthew 17:20)

The disciples had been unable to cast out a certain demon, and they asked Jesus why. He said their faith was too small. The mustard seed was the smallest of all seeds. Jesus said that even faith as small or undeveloped as a mustard seed would have been sufficient. Perhaps the disciples had tried to cast out the demon with their own ability rather than God's. It is the power of God, plus our faith, that moves mountains. There is great potential in even a little faith when we trust in God's power to act. If we feel weak or powerless as Christians, we should examine our faith, making sure we are trusting God's power, not our own ability to produce results.

If you are facing a problem that seems as big and immovable as a mountain, turn your eyes from the mountain and look to Christ for more faith. Only then will you be able to overcome the obstacles that stand in your way.

Insights:

....

....

....

....

....

....

....

It is the power of God, plus our faith, that moves mountains.

Difficulty Understanding

After they gathered again in Galilee, Jesus told them, "The Son of Man is going to be betrayed into the hands of his enemies. He will be killed, but on the third day he will be raised from the dead." And the disciples were filled with grief.

(Matthew 17:22-23)

Once again Jesus predicted His death (see also Matthew 16:21), but more important, He told of His resurrection. Unfortunately, the disciples heard only the first part of Jesus' words and became discouraged. They couldn't understand why Jesus wanted to go back to Jerusalem, where He would be killed. They had hoped that Jesus would rescue Israel from Roman control and establish a new kingdom (see Luke 24:21). Wouldn't His death be the end of all they hoped He would do?

The disciples didn't yet comprehend the purpose of Jesus' death and resurrection. They didn't know that Jesus' death and resurrection would make His Kingdom possible—a Kingdom that is "not of this world" (John 18:36). Only after His resurrection, when the Holy Spirit empowered them at Pentecost, did they begin to understand (see Acts 2).

The disciples spent three years with Jesus, saw His miracles, heard His words, and still had difficulty understanding. Despite their questions and doubts, however, they believed. Even when God's plans are difficult to understand, we, too, should believe what He has told us and trust Him to work out His plan.

Insights:
....

....

....

....

....

....

....

AND THE DISCIPLES
were filled
WITH GRIEF.

MATTHEW 17:23

Fruitless Faith?

In the morning, as Jesus was returning to Jerusalem, he was hungry,
and he noticed a fig tree beside the road. He went over to see if there
were any figs, but there were only leaves. Then he said to it, "May you
never bear fruit again!" And immediately the fig tree withered up.

(Matthew 21:18-19)

Why did Jesus curse the fig tree? Was it an angry act prompted by hunger? Despite appearances, it was not; instead, it was an acted-out parable. Jesus was showing His anger at religion without substance. The fig tree looked good from a distance, but it was fruitless on close examination. The same was true of His country's religion at the time: the Temple and its sacrifices looked impressive at first glance, but its structures and activities were hollow because they were not done to worship God sincerely (see Matthew 21:43).

Our piety might look good from a distance or at first glance but in fact be fruitless and dead. If we only appear to have faith without putting it to work in our lives, we are like the fig tree that withered and died because it bore no fruit. Genuine faith bears real spiritual fruit, such as love for God and for other people (see Galatians 5:22-23). We need to examine our own lives closely and see if our faith has fruit—if there is no fruit, we might not have genuine faith at all!

Insights:

....

....

....

....

....

....

....

....

GENUINE
FAITH
*bears real
spiritual fruit.*

Resurrection Confidence

"He isn't here! He is risen from the
dead, just as he said would happen.
Come, see where his body was lying."

(Matthew 28:6)

Jesus' resurrection is the foundation and key to the Christian faith. Why? (1) Just as Jesus promised, He rose from the dead. We can be confident, therefore, that He will accomplish everything else that He has promised. (2) Jesus' bodily resurrection shows us that He, the living Christ, is ruler of God's eternal Kingdom, not a false prophet or an impostor. (3) Because He was resurrected, we can be confident that we, too, will be resurrected as He was. Death is not the end—there is future life! (4) The power that brought Jesus back to life is available to us to bring our spiritually dead selves back to life. We can benefit from the power of His resurrection while we still live this life (see Romans 8:9-11). (5) The Resurrection is the basis for the church's witness to the world that Jesus is more than just a human leader; He is the Son of God. We can live with confidence in Jesus' resurrection, knowing that we, too, will one day be raised from the dead to live forever with Him.

Insights:

....

....

....

....

....

....

....

....

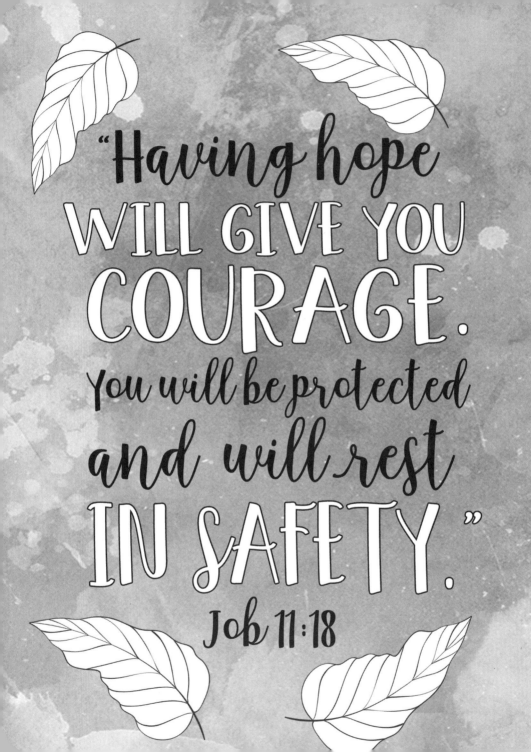

"Having hope WILL GIVE YOU COURAGE. You will be protected and will rest IN SAFETY."

Job 11:18

Following the Call

Jesus called out to them, "Come, follow me, and
I will show you how to fish for people!" And
they left their nets at once and followed him.

(Mark 1:17-18)

We sometimes assume that Jesus' disciples were great men of faith from the moment they met Jesus. They were not—they had to grow in their faith just as all believers do (see, for example, Mark 14:48-50, 66-72; John 14:1-9; 20:26-29). In fact, this occasion was not the only time Jesus called Peter (Simon), James, and John to follow Him (see Luke 5:1-11 and John 1:35-42 for the other two times). Although it took time for Jesus' call and His message to get through, the disciples followed. What set them apart was not that they had great faith right from the start but that they followed Jesus when He called them.

In the same way, we don't need to have great faith to follow Jesus—we just need to follow Him when He calls us. It doesn't take great faith to follow Him, but it does take following Him to develop great faith. We must never stop following Jesus.

Insights:

....

....

....

....

....

....

....

....

And they left
THEIR NETS
at once and
FOLLOWED HIM.
MARK 1:18

Hope for the Hopeless

A woman in the crowd had suffered for twelve years with constant bleeding. She had suffered a great deal from many doctors, and over the years she had spent everything she had to pay them, but she had gotten no better. In fact, she had gotten worse.

(Mark 5:25-26)

This woman had a seemingly incurable condition causing her to bleed constantly. This may have been a menstrual or uterine disorder that would have made her ritually unclean (Leviticus 15:25-27). Since any social contact with her would have made others unclean, she was almost completely isolated. Though her disease was probably neither contagious nor deadly, she would have been treated like a leper.

She desperately wanted Jesus to heal her, but she knew that according to Jewish law her bleeding would cause Jesus to be unclean if she touched Him. But in her desperation, she reached out in the crowd and touched the hem of His robe. Jesus justified all her hope for healing. Sometimes we feel that our problems and brokenness will keep us from God. But He is always ready to help, no matter how hopeless the situation may seem to us. We should never allow our fears to keep us from approaching Him.

Insights:

....

....

....

....

....

....

....

....

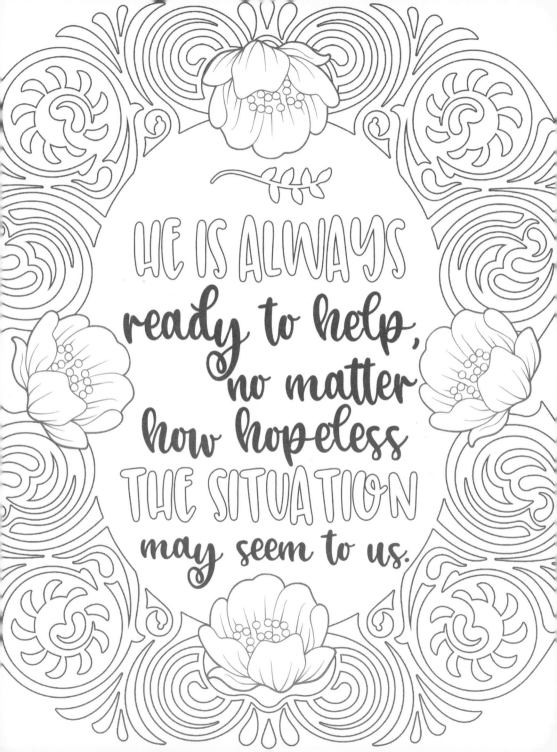

HE IS ALWAYS ready to help, no matter how hopeless THE SITUATION may seem to us.

Don't Be Afraid

They told [Jairus], "Your daughter is dead. There's no use troubling the Teacher now." But Jesus overheard them and said to Jairus, "Don't be afraid. Just have faith."

(Mark 5:35-36)

Jairus was in a severe crisis: His daughter was dying. In his desperation, he had come to Jesus, pleading with Him to heal her before it was too late. Then Jesus was delayed by a woman who touched Him and was healed. In the interim, Jairus's daughter died. No doubt Jairus felt confused, afraid, and hopeless. But then Jesus spoke to him in the midst of his crisis: "Don't be afraid. Just have faith." Jairus couldn't understand what Jesus was about to do, but he had a choice between fear and faith.

Jesus' words to Jairus in the midst of crisis speak to us as well. In Jesus, there is both hope and promise. We sometimes find ourselves in desperate situations, looking to Jesus for healing and hope. We, too, have a choice between fear and faith. The next time you feel hopeless and afraid, look to Jesus and trust Him to provide all that you need.

Insights:

....

....

....

....

....

....

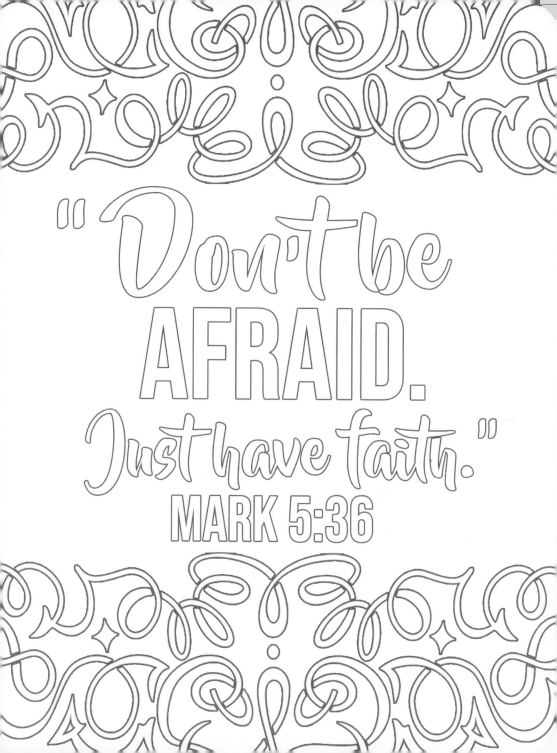

Everything Is Possible with God

[Jesus] went inside and asked, "Why all this commotion and weeping? The child isn't dead; she's only asleep." The crowd laughed at him. But he made them all leave, and he took the girl's father and mother and his three disciples into the room where the girl was lying.

(Mark 5:39-40)

The mourners laughed at Jesus when He said, "The child isn't dead; she's only asleep." They had lost all hope for her. And, in fact, the girl was dead, but Jesus had resources that the mourners knew nothing about. He described the girl as being asleep to indicate that her condition was only temporary and that she would be restored.

Jesus tolerated the crowd's abuse in order to teach an important lesson about maintaining hope and trust in Him. Today, most of the world laughs at Christ's claims. When you are belittled for expressing faith in Jesus and hope for eternal life, remember that unbelievers don't see from God's perspective. They don't understand the unlimited resources at His disposal. But we know that God is all-powerful, the ultimate giver of life.

Insights:

....

....

....

....

....

....

....

"WHY ALL this commotion AND WEEPING? The child isn't dead; SHE'S ONLY ASLEEP."

MARK 5:39

Hard Unbelief

[The disciples] still didn't understand the
significance of the miracle of the loaves.
Their hearts were too hard to take it in.

(Mark 6:52)

Even after watching Jesus miraculously feed 5,000 people, Jesus' disciples still could not take the final step of faith and believe that He was God's Son. If they had, they would not have been amazed that Jesus walked on water. The disciples' hearts were hard, perhaps because (1) they couldn't accept that this man named Jesus was really the Son of God, (2) they dared not believe that the Messiah would choose them as His followers, or (3) they still did not understand the real purpose for Jesus' coming to earth. Because they disbelieved, they did not understand.

Is your heart hardened against Jesus? Even Christians can be hard-hearted to Jesus' words. We can be informed about what His Word says, and we can be amazed at how He has worked in other people's lives, but we can refuse to believe He will come to our aid in our time of trouble. Such a reaction is not merely unbelief but a willful, hard-hearted rejection of Christ's ability to help. Instead, take courage and have faith that He is there for you.

Insights:

....

....

....

....

....

....

....

Help to Believe

"What do you mean, 'If I can'?" Jesus asked. "Anything is possible if a person believes." The father instantly cried out, "I do believe, but help me overcome my unbelief!"

(Mark 9:23-24)

Another father brought his child to Jesus' disciples for healing. This child was "possessed by an evil spirit" (Mark 9:17), and the father hoped for healing. But the disciples were unable to do the job. When Jesus returned, it became clear that the father didn't really believe that Jesus could heal the boy: "Have mercy on us and help us, if you can." That was the heart of the father's problem: He didn't yet really believe in Jesus. Jesus responded by graciously putting His finger on the problem and challenging the father to overcome it. The father cried out for help to believe, which is exactly what Jesus was giving him.

Trust and confidence, which the Bible calls *faith* (Hebrews 11:1, 6), is not something we can obtain without help. Faith is a gift from God (Ephesians 2:8-9). But Jesus knows our weaknesses and is ready to help us believe in Him. When we come to Him, we can ask Him to help us, and we can trust that no matter how small our faith is, He will help us to overcome our unbelief.

Insights:

....

....

....

....

....

....

....

Receiving Like a Child

[Jesus] said to them, "Let the children come to me. Don't stop
them! For the Kingdom of God belongs to those who are like
these children. I tell you the truth, anyone who doesn't receive
the Kingdom of God like a child will never enter it."

(Mark 10:14-15)

To feel secure, children need a loving look and a gentle touch from someone who
cares. Children believe us because they trust us. Jesus said that people should
trust in Him with this kind of childlike faith. We do not have to understand all
the mysteries of the universe; it should be enough to know that God loves us and
provides forgiveness for our sin.

How can you "receive the Kingdom of God like a child"? Adults considering
the Christian faith for the first time will have life experiences that take them
way past the ability to be literally as innocent as children. Jesus does not ask us
to put aside our experiences, but He does require a change of attitude: Adult
self-sufficiency must recognize its need for the sovereign God; adult moral defen-
siveness must humble itself before the holy God; and adult skepticism must soften
before the loving God. Children do not feel supremely powerful, perfectly righteous, or totally autonomous. These are adult fantasies. Coming to Jesus means
accepting His goodness on your behalf, confessing your need, and committing
your life to His tender guidance.

Insights:

....

....

....

....

....

....

....

"FOR THE KINGDOM OF GOD belongs to those WHO ARE LIKE these children."

Mark 10:14

Tough Love

Looking at the man, Jesus felt genuine love for him. "There is still one thing you haven't done," he told him. "Go and sell all your possessions and give the money to the poor, and you will have treasure in heaven. Then come, follow me."

(Mark 10:21)

Jesus showed tough love to the rich young man, even though Jesus knew that he might just walk away. Jesus didn't hedge on the truth. He simply offered him the chance to take part in a divine life—a life of untold riches in heaven, but also a life of self-giving and sacrifice in the present. Jesus loved this man enough to allow him to make his own decision. He didn't use force or a burden of fear to manipulate him.

Jesus loved us enough to die for us, and He also loves us enough to talk straight to us. The love He offers is unconditional, while also allowing us the freedom to follow or just walk away. He doesn't offer a superficial love akin to flattery. His love is deep and complete, and He asks us to love Him in return with the kind of love that proves itself in sacrifice.

Insights:

....

....

....

....

....

....

....

Love through Obedience

Jesus replied, "The most important commandment is this: 'Listen, O Israel! The LORD our God is the one and only LORD. And you must love the LORD your God with all your heart, all your soul, all your mind, and all your strength.' The second is equally important: 'Love your neighbor as yourself.' No other commandment is greater than these."

(Mark 12:29-31)

God's laws are not burdensome. They can be reduced to two simple principles: Love God and love others. Jesus said that if we truly love God and our neighbor, we will naturally keep all the commandments as well. This is looking at God's law positively. Rather than worrying about all we should not do, we should concentrate on all we can do to show our love for God and others.

These commands are from the Old Testament (Deuteronomy 6:5; Leviticus 19:18). When you love God completely and care for others as you care for yourself, then you have fulfilled the intent of the Ten Commandments and the other Old Testament laws. According to Jesus, these two commandments summarize all God's laws. Let them rule your thoughts, decisions, and actions. When you are uncertain about what to do, ask yourself which course of action best demonstrates love for God and love for others.

Insights:

....

....

....

....

....

....

....

Being Part of God's Plan

Then his father, Zechariah, was filled with the Holy Spirit
and gave this prophecy: "Praise the Lord, the God of Israel,
because he has visited and redeemed his people...."

(Luke 1:67-79)

Zechariah praised God with his first words after months of silence. In a song that is often called the Benedictus (after the first words in the Latin translation of this passage), Zechariah prophesied the coming of a Savior who would redeem His people and predicted that his own son, John, would prepare the Messiah's way. All the Old Testament prophecies were coming true—no wonder Zechariah praised God! The Messiah would come in Zechariah's lifetime, and his son had been chosen to pave the way.

Zechariah had just recalled hundreds of years of God's sovereign work in history, beginning with Abraham and going on into eternity. Then, in tender contrast, he personalized the story. His son had been chosen for a key role in the drama of the ages. Although God has unlimited power, He chooses to work through frail humans who begin as helpless babies. Don't minimize what God can do through those who are faithful to Him. And that includes you!

Insights:
....
....
....
....
....
....
....

Prove Your Faith

"Prove by the way you live that you have repented of your sins and turned to God. Don't just say to each other, 'We're safe, for we are descendants of Abraham.' That means nothing, for I tell you, God can create children of Abraham from these very stones."

(Luke 3:8)

Some people wanted John to baptize them so they could escape eternal punishment, but they were not really repenting from sin, nor were they willing to change the way they lived. They were more interested in observing the right rituals than in actually changing, and they believed that their status as descendants of Abraham protected them. John had harsh words for such people. He knew that God values spiritual renewal above religious ritual and that God does not play favorites but accepts anyone who lives by faith in Him.

Jesus also spoke harsh words to the respectable religious leaders. They wanted to be known as religious authorities and wanted eternal life, but they didn't want to repent of their sins. Confession of sin and a changed life are inseparable. Faith without actions is dead (James 2:14-26). Following Jesus means more than saying the right words; it means acting on what He says and letting Him change your life from the inside out.

Insights:

....

....

....

....

....

....

....

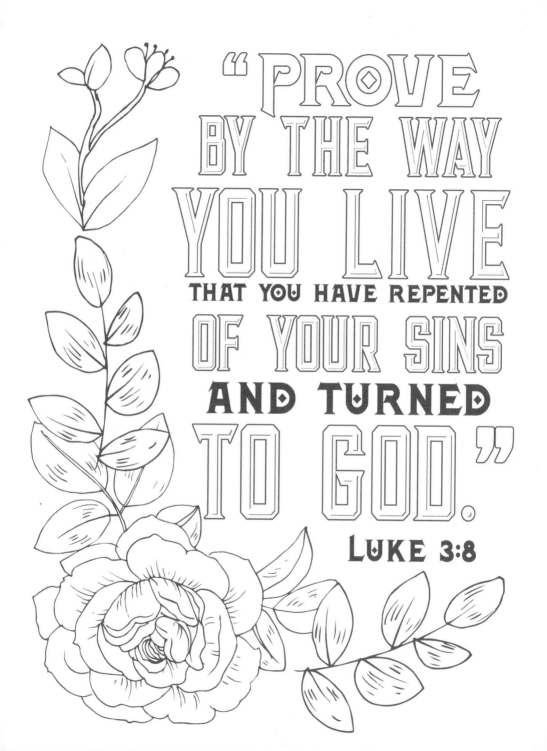

"PROVE BY THE WAY YOU LIVE THAT YOU HAVE REPENTED OF YOUR SINS AND TURNED TO GOD."

LUKE 3:8

Healing Touch

In one of the villages, Jesus met a man with an advanced
case of leprosy. When the man saw Jesus, he bowed with his
face to the ground, begging to be healed. "Lord," he said,
"if you are willing, you can heal me and make me clean."

(Luke 5:12)

Leprosy was a feared disease in Bible times because there was no known cure for it, and some forms of it were highly contagious. Leprosy had an emotional impact on people, similar to that of AIDS today. The priests monitored the disease, banishing lepers who were in a contagious stage to prevent the spread of infection and readmitting lepers whose disease was in remission.

Because leprosy destroys the nerve endings, lepers often would unknowingly damage their fingers, toes, and noses. This man with leprosy had an advanced case, so he undoubtedly had lost much bodily tissue. Still, he believed Jesus could heal him of every trace of the disease. And Jesus did just that, reaching out to touch this untouchable, contagious man in order to restore him. Jesus never refused to offer His appropriate, loving touch to people in need. We can learn from this physical demonstration of love that brought healing not just to the body but also to the soul and spirit.

Insights:

....

....

....

....

....

....

....

"IF YOU ARE WILLING, YOU CAN HEAL ME AND MAKE ME CLEAN."

Luke 5:12

Loving Your Enemies

"But to you who are willing to listen, I say, love your enemies! Do good to those who hate you. Bless those who curse you. Pray for those who hurt you."

(Luke 6:27-28)

The Jews despised the Romans because of their oppressive rule, but Jesus told His followers to love such enemies. These words caused many to turn from following Jesus. But Jesus wasn't talking about having affection for enemies; He was talking about an act of the will. You can't "fall into" this kind of love—it takes conscious effort.

Loving your enemies means acting with their best interests in mind. We can always pray for them, and we can think of ways to help them. Jesus loves the whole world, even though the world is in rebellion against God. Jesus asks us to follow His example by loving our enemies. Grant your enemies the same respect and rights as you desire for yourself.

Insights:

....

....

....

....

....

....

....

....

"Do good to those who HATE YOU."

Luke 6:27

Faith at a Distance

Turning to the crowd that was following
him, [Jesus] said, "I tell you, I haven't
seen faith like this in all Israel!"

(Luke 7:9)

A Roman army officer who heard about Jesus sent a request to Jesus on behalf of his slave who was dying. The officer may have heard about the healing of the government official's son (see John 4:46-54). He knew Jesus had the power to heal his slave. What's more, he understood that Jesus' spiritual authority over disease extended far beyond Jesus' physical presence. Just as the officer did not need to be present in order to have his own orders carried out by his subordinates, he reasoned that Jesus, too, did not need to be present in order to heal. Jesus was amazed at the officer's faith, especially because he was a Gentile who had not been brought up to know a loving God.

We sometimes forget that Jesus can act on our behalf even though He is not physically present with us. We forget that "all authority in heaven and on earth" has been given to Him (Matthew 28:18). Our faith in Him should be more like that of the government official. We can trust Jesus to do great things for us.

Insights:

....

....

....

....

....

....

....

Surprising Love

Jesus replied with a story: "A Jewish man was traveling
from Jerusalem down to Jericho, and he was attacked
by bandits. They stripped him of his clothes, beat him
up, and left him half dead beside the road. . . ."

(Luke 10:30-37)

The expert in religious law, to whom Jesus was telling this story, understood that he was commanded to love his neighbor, but he wanted to define *neighbor* in a way that excluded most people, making the command easy to follow. So Jesus told this story to demonstrate that, in fact, all people were his neighbor and that he was called to love everyone. In this story, several people came in contact with a traveler on the road to Jericho. The bandits saw him as an object to exploit; the priest saw him as a problem to avoid; and the Temple assistant saw him as an object of curiosity. Only the Samaritan, whom the Jews would have hated because of his race, treated him as a person to love.

From the parable we learn three principles about loving our neighbor: (1) lack of love is often easy to justify, even though it is never right; (2) our neighbor is anyone of any race, creed, or social background who is in need; and (3) love means acting to meet the person's need. Wherever you live, needy people are close by. There is no good reason for refusing to help.

Insights:

....

....

....

....

....

....

....

God's Estimate of Our Worth

"What is the price of five sparrows—two copper coins? Yet
God does not forget a single one of them. And the very hairs
on your head are all numbered. So don't be afraid; you are
more valuable to God than a whole flock of sparrows."

(Luke 12:6-7)

Jesus used these words to encourage people who would
soon face persecution for their commitment to Him.
Many of His followers would face judgment and separa-
tion from their families and friends because of their faith.
As they felt isolated, alone, and afraid, Jesus' words of love
must have been an amazing comfort to them. And when
we are alone and rejected by others, this reminder is a
comfort to us as well.

Our true value is God's estimate of our worth, not our
peers' estimate. Other people evaluate and categorize us
according to how we perform, what we achieve, and how
we look. But God cares for us, as He does for all of His
creatures, because we belong to Him. Thus, we can face
life without fear. We are very valuable to God.

Insights:

....

....

....

....

....

....

....

Our true value is GOD'S ESTIMATE OF OUR WORTH, not our peers' estimate.

I have chosen TO BE FAITHFUL; I HAVE DETERMINED to live by your REGULATIONS.

Psalm 119:30

Worry or Faith

*"Don't be concerned about what to eat and what to drink.
Don't worry about such things. . . . Seek the Kingdom of God
above all else, and he will give you everything you need."*

(Luke 12:29, 31)

Jesus commands us not to worry. But how can we avoid it? Only faith can free us from the anxiety caused by greed and fear. Working and planning responsibly are good; dwelling on all the ways our planning could go wrong is bad. Worry is pointless because it can't meet any of our needs; worry is foolish because the Creator of the universe loves us and knows what we need. He promises to meet all of our real needs but not necessarily all of our desires.

Overcoming worry requires two things: (1) Trust in God, your heavenly Father. This trust is expressed by praying to Him rather than worrying. (2) "Seek the Kingdom of God above all else." When we focus our attention on building God's Kingdom and advancing His purposes, we will be less likely to focus on our own problems and needs. We must put God and His purposes at the center of our lives and trust Him to take care of everything we need.

Insights:

"Seek the Kingdom of God ABOVE ALL ELSE."
Luke 12:31

Waiting to Forgive

"So [the Prodigal Son] returned home to his father. And while he was still a long way off, his father saw him coming. Filled with love and compassion, he ran to his son, embraced him, and kissed him."

(Luke 15:20)

This description comes from one of Jesus' most famous parables, the story of the lost (or prodigal) son. In this story, the son asked for his share of the family inheritance and went away to squander it on wild living. When his money ran out, the son was forced to eat with the pigs he was hired to feed. He decided he would be better off as one of his father's servants, so he went home, hoping for grace. As it turned out, the father was watching and waiting. The father had allowed his son the freedom to act foolishly, and he had let him suffer the consequences. But the father was also ready to welcome his son when he chose to return.

This is really a story about all of us. God's love is constant and patient and welcoming. He will search for us and give us opportunities to respond, but He will not force us to come to Him. Like the father in this story, God waits patiently for us to come to our senses and humbly return. He is eagerly waiting to welcome and forgive us.

Insights:
....

....

....

....

....

....

....

HE IS EAGERLY *waiting* TO WELCOME *and forgive* US.

A Stubborn Cry for Help

As Jesus approached Jericho, a blind beggar was sitting beside the road. . . . They told him that Jesus the Nazarene was going by. So he began shouting, "Jesus, Son of David, have mercy on me!"

(Luke 18:35-38)

Beggars often would wait along the roads near cities because that was where the most people would see them. Usually disabled in some way, these beggars were unable to earn a living in the normal way. Medical help was not available for their problems, and people tended to ignore their obligation to care for the needy (Leviticus 25:35-38). Thus, the only way to get noticed was to sit by the road and make some noise. They had little hope of escaping their degraded way of life.

But this blind beggar found hope in the Messiah. He shamelessly cried out for Jesus' attention, even when the people nearby tried to stop him. And by stubbornly continuing to cry for help, he demonstrated his hope in Jesus, who healed him and said, "Your faith has healed you" (Luke 18:42). No matter how desperate your situation may seem, call out to Jesus in faith—and keep on calling out. He will bring the help you need.

Insights:

....

....

....

....

....

....

....

Call out TO JESUS in faith— AND KEEP ON calling out.

Faith Changes Everything

Zacchaeus stood before the Lord and said, "I will give half my wealth to the poor, Lord, and if I have cheated people on their taxes, I will give them back four times as much!" Jesus responded, "Salvation has come to this home today, for this man has shown himself to be a true son of Abraham."

(Luke 19:8-9)

Judging from the crowd's reaction to him, Zacchaeus must have been a very crooked tax collector. When Jesus said Zacchaeus was a son of Abraham and yet was lost, He must have shocked His hearers in at least two ways: (1) they would not want to hear that this unpopular tax collector was a fellow son of Abraham, and (2) they would not want to admit that sons of Abraham could be lost. But a person is not saved because of a good heritage or condemned by a bad one. Jesus came to save all the lost, regardless of their background or previous way of life. Through faith, the lost can be forgiven and made new.

After Zacchaeus met Jesus, he realized that his life needed straightening out. By giving to the poor and making fourfold restitution—just as God commanded (see Exodus 22:1)—Zacchaeus demonstrated inner change by outward action. Following Jesus in your head or heart alone is not enough. You must show your faith by changed behavior. Has your faith resulted in action? What changes do you need to make?

Insights:

....

....

....

....

....

....

....

The Messiah's Identity

Then Jesus presented them with a question. "Why is it," he asked, "that the Messiah is said to be the son of David?"

(Luke 20:41)

The Pharisees and Sadducees had asked their questions, but they had been unable to confound Jesus. When they ran out of questions, Jesus turned the tables and asked them a question that went right to the heart of the matter—what they thought about the Messiah's identity. The Pharisees knew that the Messiah would be a descendant of David, but they expected only a human ruler to restore Israel's greatness as in the days of David and Solomon. They did not understand that the Messiah would be more than a human descendant—He would be God in the flesh. Jesus quoted from Psalm 110:1 to show that the Messiah would be both human and divine. But His listeners were unable to comprehend; the Pharisees and Sadducees remained confused over Jesus' identity.

The central issue of life is what we believe about Jesus. Other spiritual questions are secondary. Do we believe that Jesus is who He said He is—the Son of God, who is Himself God?

Insights:

....

....

....

....

....

....

....

Reaching Love

"For this is how God loved the world: He gave his one and
only Son, so that everyone who believes in him will not perish
but have eternal life. God sent his Son into the world not
to judge the world, but to save the world through him."

(John 3:16-17)

The message of the Good News comes into focus in this verse. God's
love is not static or self-centered; it reaches out and draws others in.
Here God sets the pattern of true love, the basis for all love relationships—when you love someone dearly, you are willing to give
freely to the point of self-sacrifice. God paid dearly with the life of
His Son, the highest price He could pay. Jesus accepted our punishment, paid the price for our sins, and then offered us the new life
He had bought for us.

When we share the Good News with others, our love must be
like Jesus'—willingly giving up our own comfort and security so
that others might join us in receiving God's love. It isn't about being
successful in God's Kingdom. It isn't about us at all. It's all about
telling others the story of Jesus and allowing others to be confronted
and transformed by His love.

Insights:

....

....

....

....

....

....

....

....

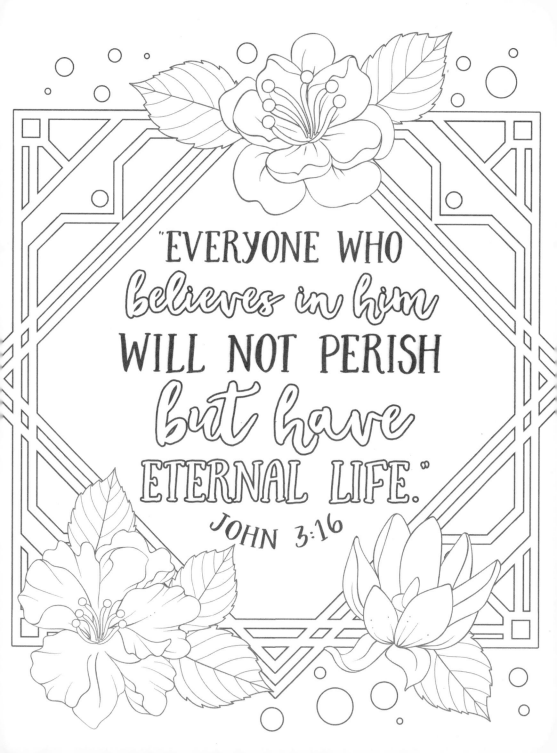

True and False Hope

A large crowd of Passover visitors took palm branches and went down
the road to meet him. They shouted, "Praise God! Blessings on the
one who comes in the name of the LORD! Hail to the King of Israel!"

(John 12:12-13)

Jesus began His last week on earth by riding into Jerusalem on a donkey under a canopy of palm branches, with crowds hailing Him as their king. But most of the people praising God for giving them a king had the wrong idea about Jesus. They were sure He would be a national leader who would restore their nation to its former glory and bring them the good life. Thus, they were deaf to the words of their prophets and blind to Jesus' real mission. They had expectations built on false hopes. When it became apparent that Jesus was not going to fulfill their hopes, many people turned against Him.

What are your expectations of Jesus? Do you expect Him to make you happy no matter what? Do you expect Him to make sure nothing bad ever happens to you? Like the people in ancient Israel, you may be placing unrealistic expectations on Him. God's plan for your life could include many blessings, but it will almost certainly include suffering and heartache as well. Following Jesus includes the idea of picking up your cross. But one thing is for certain—no matter what you face in life, Jesus will be with you through it. That is a hope you can count on.

Insights:

....

....

....

....

....

....

....

Sharing Our Faith

Many people did believe in him, however, including some
of the Jewish leaders. But they wouldn't admit it for fear that
the Pharisees would expel them from the synagogue. For
they loved human praise more than the praise of God.

(John 12:42-43)

Many of the people who saw and heard Jesus refused to believe in Him, despite seeing Him perform many miraculous signs that demonstrated that He was genuinely empowered by God. There were others, though, who did believe, but they were afraid to admit it. They remembered that the man who had been healed of his blindness had been expelled from the synagogue (John 9), and they did not want to suffer the same kind of ostracism and social isolation. The Jewish leaders were concerned for their very livelihood, which depended on their prestigious position in the synagogue, and admitting that they believed in Jesus would jeopardize all that they had in this world.

John's Gospel has strong words for such people: "They loved human praise more than the praise of God" (John 12:43). It can be difficult to admit that we believe in Jesus, especially when the social and even physical costs can be high. But the praise of other people is fickle and short-lived, whereas God's Kingdom is eternal. We should be much more concerned about God's eternal acceptance than about the temporary approval of other people.

Insights:

....

....

....

....

....

....

....

MANY PEOPLE DID BELIEVE IN HIM, *however*, INCLUDING SOME *of the Jewish* LEADERS.

John 12:42

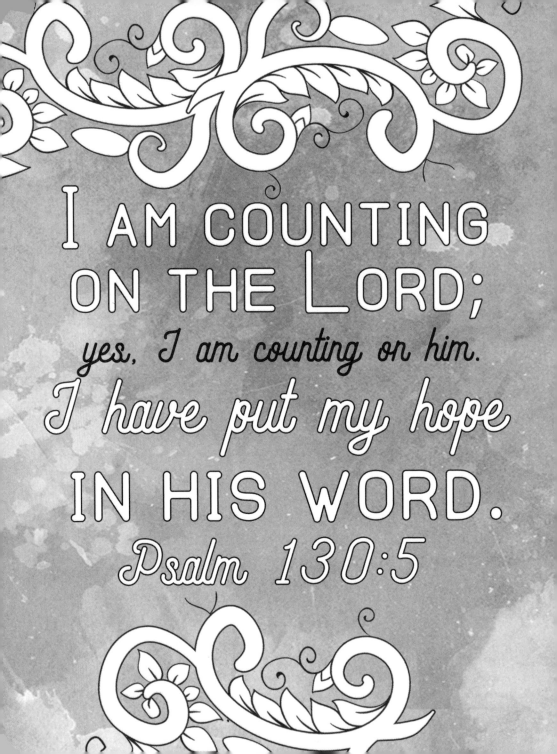

I AM COUNTING ON THE LORD; yes, I am counting on him. I have put my hope IN HIS WORD. Psalm 130:5

Marked by Love

"So now I am giving you a new commandment: Love each other.
Just as I have loved you, you should love each other. Your love for
one another will prove to the world that you are my disciples."

(John 13:34-35)

Jesus says we should love each other just as He loves us. Our love for one another will prove we are His disciples. Do people see petty bickering, jealousy, and division in your church? Or do they know you are Jesus' followers by your love for one another? Christians will get plenty of hatred from the world; from each other we need love and support. Do you allow small problems to get in the way of loving other believers? Jesus commands that you love them, and He will give you the strength to do it.

Love is more than simply warm feelings; it is an attitude that reveals itself in action. How can we love others as Jesus loves us? By helping when it's not convenient, by giving when it hurts, by devoting energy to others' welfare rather than our own, by absorbing hurts from others without complaining or fighting back. This kind of loving is hard to do. That is why people notice when you do it and know you are empowered by a supernatural source.

Insights:

....

....

....

....

....

....

....

"Just as I have LOVED YOU, YOU SHOULD LOVE EACH OTHER."

John 13:34

Loving Others First

"This is my commandment: Love each other in the
same way I have loved you. There is no greater love
than to lay down one's life for one's friends."

(John 15:12-13)

To love others was not a new commandment (see Leviticus 19:18), but to love others as much as Christ loved others was revolutionary! Now we are to love others based on Jesus' sacrificial love for us. Such love will not only bring unbelievers to Christ; it will also keep believers strong and united in a world hostile to God. Jesus was a living example of God's love, as we are to be living examples of Jesus' love.

Jesus loved us enough to give His life for us. We may not have to die for someone else, but there are other ways to practice sacrificial love: listening, helping, encouraging, giving. Think of someone who needs this kind of love today. Give them all the love you can, and then try to give a little more.

Insights:

....

....

....

....

....

....

....

....

Stages of Faith

Early on Sunday morning, while it was still dark, Mary Magdalene came to the tomb
and found that the stone had been rolled away from the entrance. She ran and found
Simon Peter and the other disciple, the one whom Jesus loved. She said, "They have
taken the Lord's body out of the tomb, and we don't know where they have put him!"

(John 20:1-2)

When Mary first saw Jesus' empty tomb, she did not immediately
understand that He had risen from the dead. Instead, she thought that
someone had robbed the tomb and taken Jesus' body. It was only later,
when Jesus Himself appeared to her, that she began to comprehend
what had taken place (see John 20:11-18).

Like Mary and the disciples, we also pass through stages on the way
to faith. At first we may think the story is a fabrication, impossible to
believe (John 20:2). Like Peter, we may check out the facts and still be
puzzled (John 20:6). Only when we encounter Jesus personally are we
able to accept His resurrection (John 20:16). Then, as we commit ourselves to the risen Lord and devote our lives to serving Him, we begin
to understand fully the reality of His presence with us (John 20:28).
Wherever we are in our journey of faith, we can take the next step by
asking Jesus to make Himself real to us.

Insights:

....

....

....

....

....

....

....

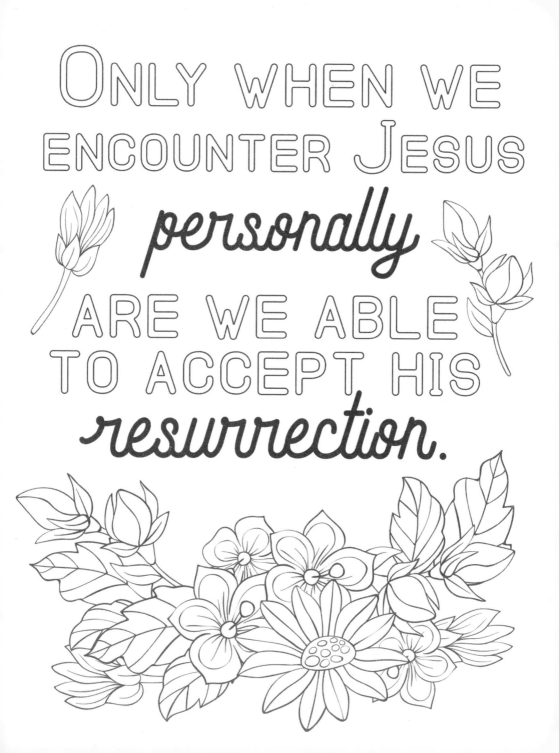

Loving Proof

After breakfast Jesus asked Simon Peter, "Simon son of John, do
you love me more than these?" "Yes, Lord," Peter replied, "you
know I love you." "Then feed my lambs," Jesus told him.

(John 21:15)

In this beach scene, Jesus led Peter through an experience that would
remove the cloud of his denial. Peter had denied Jesus three times.
Three times Jesus asked Peter if he loved Him. When Peter answered
yes, Jesus told him to feed His sheep. It is one thing to say you love
Jesus, but the real test is in your willingness to serve Him. Peter had
repented, and here Jesus was asking him to commit his life through
action.

Peter's life changed when he finally realized who Jesus was. His
occupation changed from fisherman to evangelist. His identity
changed from being impetuous to being a "rock." And his relationship to Jesus changed—he was forgiven, and he finally understood
the significance of Jesus' words about His death and resurrection.
We also have denied Jesus, and Jesus also comes to us with this question: "Do you love Me?" We can prove our answer by how we live.

Insights:

....

....

....

....

....

....

....

Faith Based on Fact

During the forty days after he suffered and died, [Jesus]
appeared to the apostles from time to time, and he proved
to them in many ways that he was actually alive. And
he talked to them about the Kingdom of God.

(Acts 1:3)

Jesus' disciples were eyewitnesses to all that had happened to Jesus—His life before His crucifixion and the forty days after His resurrection as He taught them more about the Kingdom of God. Today people still doubt Jesus' resurrection. But Jesus appeared to the disciples on many occasions after His resurrection, proving that He was alive.

Consider the change the Resurrection made in the disciples' lives. At Jesus' death, they had scattered, feeling disillusioned and fearing for their lives. After seeing the resurrected Christ, they became fearless and risked everything to spread the Good News about Him around the world. They faced imprisonment, beatings, rejection, and martyrdom, yet they never compromised their mission. These men would not have risked—and, in some cases, given—their lives for something they knew was a fraud. They knew Jesus was alive, and the early church was on fire with their enthusiasm to tell others.

We, too, need to know the facts of Jesus' resurrection so that we can have confidence in the apostles' testimony. More than twenty centuries later, we can still be confident that our faith is based on fact.

Insights:

....

....

....

....

....

....

....

....

And he talked TO THEM ABOUT the Kingdom of God.

ACTS 1:3

Right Relationship with God

This Good News tells us how God makes us right
in his sight. This is accomplished from start to
finish by faith. As the Scriptures say, "It is through
faith that a righteous person has life."

(Romans 1:17)

The Good News is the message that Jesus died to take away our sins and rose from the dead to give us new life and that we are acceptable to God on the basis of believing the message, not on the basis of the things that we do (see also Romans 3:28). The Good News shows us how righteous God is in His plan for us to be saved and how we may be made fit for eternal life.

Why does God save us by faith alone? The fact is that we can't keep the law or measure up to God's standards—we cannot save ourselves; we need Him to save us. Faith exalts what God has done, not what we do. God wants a relationship with us based on our faith in who He is and what He has done. When we trust Christ, our relationship with God is made right. From start to finish, God declares us to be righteous because of faith and faith alone. As we trust God, we are saved—we have life both now and forever.

Insights:

....

....

....

....

....

....

....

"IT IS THROUGH FAITH THAT A RIGHTEOUS PERSON HAS LIFE."

ROMANS 1:17

Declared "Not Guilty"

> For everyone has sinned; we all fall short of God's glorious standard. Yet God, in his grace, freely makes us right in his sight. He did this through Christ Jesus when he freed us from the penalty for our sins.
>
> *(Romans 3:23-24)*

Some sins seem bigger than others because their obvious consequences are much more serious. Murder, for example, seems to us to be worse than hatred, and adultery seems worse than pride. But this does not mean that because we only commit "little" sins we deserve eternal life. All sins make us sinners, and all sins cut us off from our holy God. All sins, therefore, lead to death (because they disqualify us from living with God), regardless of how great or small they seem. Don't minimize "little" sins or overrate "big" sins. They all separate us from God, but they all can be forgiven.

Paul explains that God declares us righteous. When a judge in a court of law declares the defendant not guilty, all the charges are removed from his record. Legally, it is as if the person had never been accused. When God forgives our sins, our record is wiped clean. From His perspective, it is as though we had never sinned. He could do this because Jesus took the penalty we deserved. Christ purchased our freedom from sin, and the price was His life.

Insights:

....

....

....

....

....

....

....

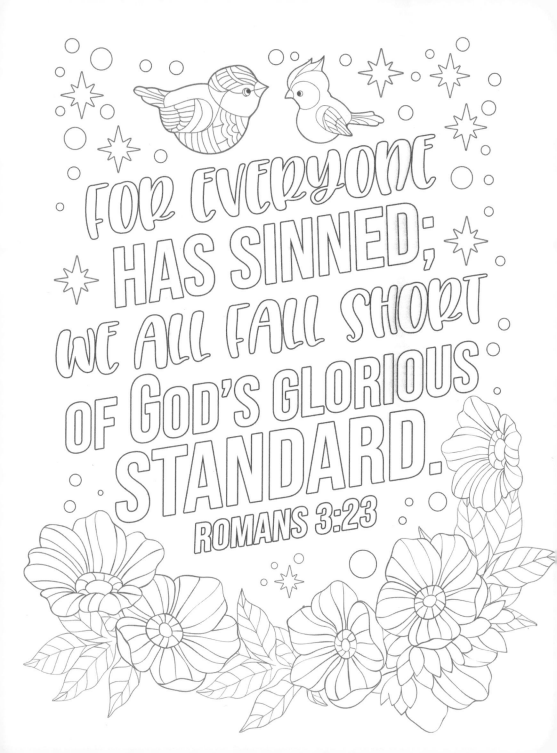

Trust in God's Promises

Abraham never wavered in believing God's promise. In fact, his
faith grew stronger, and in this he brought glory to God. He was
fully convinced that God is able to do whatever he promises. And
because of Abraham's faith, God counted him as righteous.

(Romans 4:20-22)

Abraham never doubted that God would fulfill His promise. Abraham's life
was marked by mistakes, sins, and failures, as well as by wisdom and goodness,
but he consistently trusted God. His faith was strengthened by the obstacles he
faced, and his life was an example of faith in action. If he had looked only at
his own resources for subduing Canaan and founding a nation, he would have
given up in despair. But Abraham looked to God, obeyed Him, and waited for
God to fulfill His word.

Abraham is an example for how we should follow God by faith—in fact,
all those who have a faith relationship with God through Christ are called
"children of Abraham" (see Galatians 3:7, 29). Like Abraham, we have received
God's promises—that God has taken away our sins through Christ, that He
has given us His Holy Spirit to fill us and guide us, and that He will receive us
into His eternal Kingdom if we continue to follow Him by faith. We should,
like Abraham, be fully convinced that God will do what He has promised.

Insights:

....

....

....

....

....

....

....

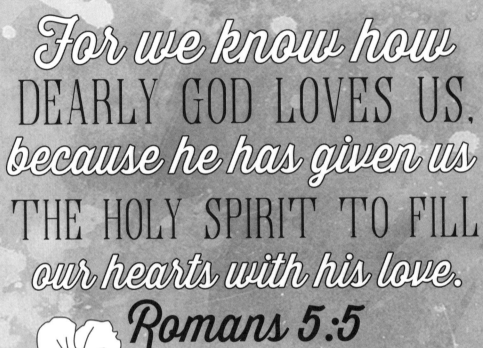

For we know how DEARLY GOD LOVES US, because he has given us THE HOLY SPIRIT TO FILL our hearts with his love. Romans 5:5

Hope through Suffering

We can rejoice, too, when we run into problems and trials,
for we know that they help us develop endurance. And
endurance develops strength of character, and character strengthens our confident hope of salvation.

(Romans 5:3-4)

For first-century Christians, suffering was the rule rather than the exception. Paul tells us that in the future we will become victors over sin and death, but until then we must overcome the challenges of this life. This means we will experience difficulties that help us grow. We rejoice in suffering, not because we like pain or deny its tragedy, but because we know God is using life's difficulties and Satan's attacks to build our character.

There is hope attached to our suffering. The problems we run into will develop our perseverance—which in turn will strengthen our character, deepen our trust in God, and give us greater confidence about the future. You probably find your patience tested in some way every day. Thank God for those opportunities to grow, and deal with them in His strength (see also James 1:2-4; 1 Peter 1:6-7).

Insights:

....

....

....

....

....

....

....

....

There is hope
ATTACHED
TO OUR
suffering.

Eager for Freedom

All creation is waiting eagerly for that future day when God will reveal who his children really are. Against its will, all creation was subjected to God's curse. But with eager hope, the creation looks forward to the day when it will join God's children in glorious freedom from death and decay.

(Romans 8:19-21)

Christians see the world as it is—physically decaying and spiritually infected with sin. But Christians do not need to be pessimistic because they have hope for future glory. They look forward to the new heaven and new earth that God has promised, and they wait for God's new order that will free the world from sin, sickness, and evil. In the meantime, Christians go with Christ into the world, where they heal people's bodies and souls and fight the evil effects of sin in the world.

Sin has caused all creation to fall from the perfect state in which God created it. The world is in bondage to death and decay so that it cannot fulfill its intended purpose. One day all creation will be liberated and transformed. Until that time it waits in eager expectation for the resurrection of God's children.

Insights:

....

....

....

....

....

....

....

....

Confident Hope

We were given this hope when we were saved. (If
we already have something, we don't need to hope
for it. But if we look forward to something we don't
yet have, we must wait patiently and confidently.)

(Romans 8:24-25)

In Romans, Paul presents the idea that salvation is past, present, and future.
It is past because we were saved the moment we believed in Jesus Christ as
Savior (Romans 3:21-26; 5:1-11; 6:1-11, 22-23); our new life (eternal life)
begins at that moment. And salvation is present because we are being saved;
this is the process of sanctification. But at the same time, we have not fully
received all the benefits and blessings of salvation that will be ours when
Christ's new Kingdom is completely established. That's our future salvation.

While we can be confident of our salvation, we still look ahead with hope
and trust toward that complete change of body and personality that lies
beyond this life, when we will be like Christ (1 John 3:2). What exactly are
we waiting for? New bodies, a new heaven and new earth, rest and rewards,
our eternal family and home, the absence of sin and suffering, and being
face-to-face with Jesus! We can live with confident hope that God will make
it happen in His perfect timing and wisdom.

Insights:

....

....

....

....

....

....

....

....

Everything Works Together for Good

And we know that God causes everything to work together for the good of
those who love God and are called according to his purpose for them. For
God knew his people in advance, and he chose them to become like his Son,
so that his Son would be the firstborn among many brothers and sisters.

(Romans 8:28-29)

God works in everything—not just isolated incidents—for our good.
Evil is prevalent in our fallen world, but God is able to turn every circumstance around for our good. Note that God is working not to make
us happy but to fulfill His purpose for us—to make us like Christ (1 John
3:2). As we become more and more like Him, we discover our true selves,
the people we were created to be. How can we become like Christ? By
reading and obeying Scripture, by studying His life on earth through the
Gospels, by spending time in prayer, by being filled with His Spirit, and
by doing His work in the world.

And notice that this promise is not for everybody. It can be claimed
only by those who love God and are called by Him—that is, those who
belong to Jesus Christ. Such people have a new perspective, a new mind-
set. They trust in God, not in worldly treasures; their security is in heaven,
not on earth. Their faith in God does not waver in pain and persecution
because they know God is with them.

Insights:

....

....

....

....

....

....

....

....

Unconquerable Love

Nothing can ever separate us from God's love. Neither death nor life, neither angels nor demons, neither our fears for today nor our worries about tomorrow—not even the powers of hell can separate us from God's love. . . . Indeed, nothing in all creation will ever be able to separate us from the love of God that is revealed in Christ Jesus our Lord.

(Romans 8:38-39)

These verses contain one of the most comforting promises in all Scripture. Believers have always had to face hardships in many forms: persecution, illness, imprisonment, and even death. These sometimes cause them to fear that they have been abandoned by Christ. But this passage reaffirms God's profound love for His people. No matter what happens to us, no matter where we are, we can never be separated from His love.

Suffering should not drive us away from God but should help us to identify with Him and allow His love to heal us. Whatever situation you find yourself in today, take this truth to heart. Nothing can separate us from Christ's presence. His death for us is proof of His unconquerable love. God tells us how great His love is so that we will feel totally secure in Him. If we believe these overwhelming assurances, we will not be afraid.

Insights:

....

....

....

....

....

....

....

Honoring Each Other

Don't just pretend to love others. Really love
them. Hate what is wrong. Hold tightly to what
is good. Love each other with genuine affection, and take delight in honoring each other.

(Romans 12:9-10)

We can honor others in one of two ways. One involves ulterior motives. We honor our bosses so they will reward us, our employees so they will work harder, the wealthy so they will contribute to our cause, the powerful so they will use their power for us and not against us. But God's way involves love. As Christians, we honor people because they have been created in God's image, because they are our brothers and sisters in Christ, and because they have a unique contribution to make to Christ's church.

Does God's way of honoring others sound too difficult for your competitive nature? Genuine love requires concentration and effort. It means helping others become better people. It demands our time, money, and personal involvement. No individual has the capacity to express love to a whole community, but the body of Christ in your town does. Look for people who need your love, and look for ways you and your fellow believers can love your community for Christ. Why not try to outdo one another in showing honor? Put others first!

Insights:

....

....

....

....

....

....

....

DON'T JUST *pretend* TO LOVE OTHERS. *Really love* THEM.
ROMANS 12:9

Love Your Neighbor

Owe nothing to anyone—except for your obligation to love one another. If you love your neighbor,
you will fulfill the requirements of God's law.

(Romans 13:8)

Why is love for others called an obligation? We are permanently in debt to Christ for the lavish love He has poured out on us. The only way we can even begin to repay this debt is by fulfilling our obligation to love others in turn. Because Christ's love will always be infinitely greater than ours, we will always have the obligation to love our neighbors.

But look closely at how the command to love is given: "Love your neighbor as yourself" (Romans 13:9). Think about it. Even if you have low self-esteem, you probably don't willingly let yourself go hungry. You take care of your body and may even exercise. You clothe yourself reasonably well, at least enough to stay warm. You make sure there's a roof over your head. You try not to let yourself be cheated or injured. This is the kind of love we need to have for our neighbors. Do we see that others are fed, clothed, and housed as well as they can be? Loving others means actively working to see that their needs are met. Each day look for one thing you can do to improve the life of another person. If no one you know needs help, look for some new friends!

Insights:

....

....

....

....

....

....

....

Weak and Strong Faith

Accept other believers who are weak in
faith, and don't argue with them about
what they think is right or wrong.

(Romans 14:1)

Who is weak in faith, and who is strong? Our faith is strong in an area if we can survive contact with worldly people without falling into their patterns. It is weak in an area if we must avoid certain activities, people, or places in order to protect our spiritual lives. We are all weak in some areas and strong in others. It is important to take self-inventory in order to find out our strengths and weaknesses. Whenever we are in doubt, we should ask, "Can I do that without sinning? Can I influence others for good rather than being influenced by them?"

In areas of strength, we should not fear being defiled by the world; rather, we should go and serve God. In areas of weakness, we need to be cautious. If we have a weak faith but expose it, we are being foolish. At the same time, if we have a strong faith but shelter it, we are not doing Christ's work in the world. In all things, we need to consider our own strengths and weaknesses and trust Christ to lead us to do what is best.

Insights:

....

....

....

....

....

....

....

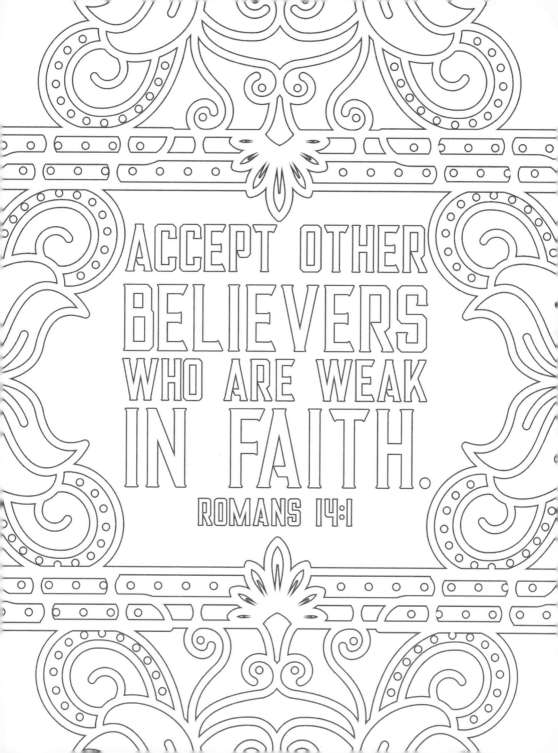

Free to Love

If what I eat causes another believer to sin, I will
never eat meat again as long as I live—for I don't
want to cause another believer to stumble.

(1 Corinthians 8:13)

Christian freedom does not mean that anything goes. It means that our salvation is not obtained by good deeds or legalistic rules; it is the free gift of God (Ephesians 2:8-9). Christian freedom, then, is inseparably tied to Christian responsibility. New believers are often very sensitive to what is right or wrong, what they should or shouldn't do. Some actions may be perfectly all right for us to do but may harm a Christian brother or sister who is still young in the faith and learning what the Christian life is all about.

We must be careful not to offend more sensitive Christians or, by our example, cause them to sin. When we love others, our freedom should be less important to us than strengthening their faith and meeting their needs. Love always calls us to use the needs of others to guide our actions. Sometimes we may need to give up doing something or going somewhere for the good of the Christian community we participate in.

Insights:

....

....

....

....

....

....

....

Dealing with Temptation

The temptations in your life are no different from what others
experience. And God is faithful. He will not allow the temptation to be more than you can stand. When you are tempted,
he will show you a way out so that you can endure.

(1 Corinthians 10:13)

In a culture filled with moral depravity and sin-inducing pressures,
Paul encouraged the Corinthians about temptation. He said that
(1) temptations happen to everyone, so don't feel you've been sin-
gled out; (2) others have resisted temptation, and so can you; and
(3) any temptation can be resisted because God will show you a way
out. Paul wanted you to know that no matter how strong the temptations you face are, you can have hope.

So how does God show you a way out? God equips you to resist
temptation by helping you (1) recognize those people and situations
that give you trouble, (2) run from anything you know is wrong,
(3) choose to do only what is right, (4) pray for God's help, and
(5) seek friends who love God and can offer help when you are
tempted. Running from a tempting situation is your first step on the
way to victory (see 2 Timothy 2:22).

Insights:

....

....

....

....

....

....

....

God
is faithful.
1 CORINTHIANS 10:13

Power of Love

If I could speak all the languages of earth and of angels, but didn't love others, I would only be a noisy gong or a clanging cymbal.

(1 Corinthians 13:1)

In 1 Corinthians 12, Paul shows how the Corinthians lacked love in how they used their spiritual gifts. Chapter 13 defines what real love is, and then chapter 14 shows how love works. Love is more important than all the spiritual gifts exercised in the church body. Great faith, acts of service, or miracle-working power have little effect without love. In fact, they can do more damage than good.

Love makes our actions and gifts useful because it awakens us to what the recipients really need. Have you seen spiritual gifts demonstrated (preaching, prophecy, service, giving) that drew attention only to the person offering the gift? Often in such cases, no one is really helped—except perhaps the reputation of the giver. But if love informs what we do, gifts are offered with concern for the recipients, and the giver becomes invisible. This is the power of love, and unlike the spiritual gifts, love is available to everyone.

Insights:

....

....

....

....

....

....

....

....

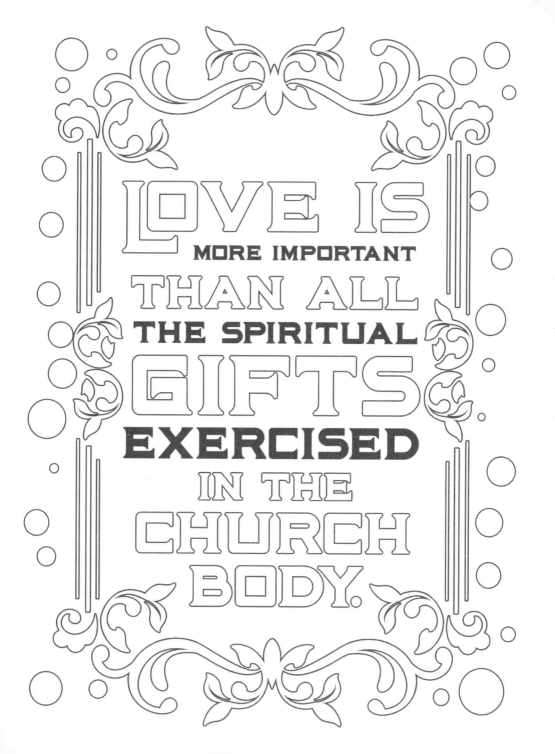

LOVE IS MORE IMPORTANT THAN ALL THE SPIRITUAL GIFTS EXERCISED IN THE CHURCH BODY.

Love Is Generous

Love is patient and kind. Love is not jealous or boastful or proud or rude. It does not demand its own way. It is not irritable, and it keeps no record of being wronged. It does not rejoice about injustice but rejoices whenever the truth wins out. Love never gives up, never loses faith, is always hopeful, and endures through every circumstance.

(1 Corinthians 13:4-7)

Our society is confused about what love really is, often mistaking lust for love. Lust is all about seeking personal pleasure with no thought for anyone else. Lust is never patient or kind. It is almost always jealous, boastful, proud, and rude. It always demands its own way. It is almost always irritable, and it will always keep a record of wrongs. That's because lust is self-centered to its core.

Unlike lust, God's kind of love is directed outward toward others, not inward toward ourselves. It is utterly unselfish and generous. This kind of love goes against our natural inclinations. It is impossible to have this love unless God helps us set aside our own natural desires so that we can love and not expect anything in return. Thus, the more we become like Christ, the more love we will show to others.

Insights:

....

....

....

....

....

....

....

....

Love is patient and kind.

1 Corinthians 13:4

Faith Expressed by Love

Three things will last forever—
faith, hope, and love—and the
greatest of these is love.

(1 Corinthians 13:13)

Paul wrote that love endures forever. In morally corrupt Corinth, love had become a mixed-up term with little meaning. Today, people are still confused about love. Love is the greatest of all human qualities and is an attribute of God Himself (1 John 4:8). Love involves unselfish service to others. Faith is the foundation and content of God's message; hope is the attitude and focus; love is the action.

When faith and hope are in line, you are free to love completely because you understand how God loves. Does your faith fully express itself in loving others? If our faith doesn't show itself in loving actions, we should seriously question whether it is true faith. Faith always demonstrates itself with acts of unselfish love.

Insights:

....

....

....

....

....

....

....

Promised Presence

If our hope in Christ is only for this life, we are more to be pitied than anyone in the world. But in fact, Christ has been raised from the dead. He is the first of a great harvest of all who have died.

(1 Corinthians 15:19-20)

Why does Paul say believers would be "more to be pitied than anyone in the world" if there were only earthly value to Christianity? In Paul's day, Christianity often brought a person persecution, ostracism from family, and, in many cases, poverty. There were few tangible benefits from being a Christian in that society. It was certainly not a step up the social or career ladder. Even today in many nations around the world, being a Christian is a definite mark against you. It can even cost you your life.

If what Christians believe is a lie, we would be pitiful because we would be going through such suffering for no purpose. Fortunately, that is not the case! We have hope in this life and the next because Jesus Christ rose from the dead and has promised His constant presence with us now and eternal life later.

Insights:

....

....

....

....

....

....

....

HE IS THE FIRST OF A GREAT HARVEST OF ALL WHO HAVE DIED.
1 CORINTHIANS 15:20

Death Swallowed in Victory

Then, when our dying bodies have been transformed into bodies that will never die, this Scripture will be fulfilled: "Death is swallowed up in victory. O death, where is your victory? O death, where is your sting?"

(1 Corinthians 15:54-55)

Satan seemed to be victorious in the Garden of Eden (Genesis 3). The consequences of Adam and Eve's sin brought a curse against them and all their descendants—including us. And Satan also seemed victorious at the cross of Jesus. As Jesus hung dying on the cross with darkness filling the sky, it seemed that evil had won the battle. But God turned Satan's apparent victory into defeat when Jesus Christ rose from the dead (Colossians 2:15; Hebrews 2:14-15).

So now death is no longer a source of dread or fear. Christ overcame it, and someday we will also. The law will no longer make sinners out of us just because we cannot keep it. Death has been defeated, and we have hope beyond the grave through Christ. We have the promise of an eternal, resurrected life in the presence of our loving Father.

Insights:

....

....

....

....

....

....

....

We have hope BEYOND the grave THROUGH Christ.

Success through Suffering

We are pressed on every side by troubles, but we are not
crushed. We are perplexed, but not driven to despair.
We are hunted down, but never abandoned by God.
We get knocked down, but we are not destroyed.

(2 Corinthians 4:8-9)

Paul reminds us that though we may think we are at the end of our rope,
we should never be without hope. Our perishable bodies are subject to
sin and suffering, but God never abandons us. Because Christ has won
the victory over death, we have eternal life. All our risks, humiliations,
and trials are opportunities for Christ to demonstrate His power and
presence in and through us. No matter how badly things may be going in
a human sense, God is present with us each step of the way.

We often think when things aren't going well for us that God has
abandoned us. The success syndrome is a great enemy of effective Christian living. From an earthly perspective, Paul (the writer of these verses)
was not very successful. Like him, we must carry out our lives, looking to
God for strength. When opposition, slander, or disappointment threat-
ens to rob you of the victory, remember that no one can destroy what
God has accomplished through you.

Insights:

....

....

....

....

....

....

....

....

PURSUE RIGHTEOUSNESS AND A GODLY LIFE,

along with faith,

love,

perseverance,

and gentleness.

1 TIMOTHY 6:11

Finding the Silver Lining

For our present troubles are small and won't last very long. . . . So
we don't look at the troubles we can see now; rather, we fix our
gaze on things that cannot be seen. For the things we see now will
soon be gone, but the things we cannot see will last forever.

(2 Corinthians 4:17-18)

Our troubles should not diminish our faith or disillusion
us. We should realize there is a purpose in our suffering.
Problems and human limitations have several benefits:
(1) they remind us of Christ's suffering for us; (2) they
keep us from pride; (3) they cause us to look beyond
this brief life; (4) they give us opportunities to prove
our faith to others; and (5) they give God the opportunity to demonstrate His power. See your troubles as
opportunities!

Our ultimate hope when we are experiencing terrible
illness, persecution, or pain is the realization that this
life is not all there is—there is life after death! Knowing
that we will live forever with Jesus in a place without sin
and suffering can help us live above the pain we face in
this life.

Insights:

....

....

....

....

....

....

....

....

WE FIX OUR GAZE ON THINGS THAT CANNOT BE SEEN.

2 Corinthians 4:18

Dying to Live

While we live in these earthly bodies, we groan and sigh,
but it's not that we want to die and get rid of these bodies
that clothe us. Rather, we want to put on our new bodies
so that these dying bodies will be swallowed up by life.

(2 Corinthians 5:4)

Paul's knowledge that his dying body would be swallowed up by eternal life is a hope that we all can share. According to the writer of Ecclesiastes, God "has planted eternity in the human heart" (Ecclesiastes 3:11). Human beings have an innate sense of transcendence and a longing for ultimate reality—things that can be experienced only in the eternal presence of God. This spiritual desire is addressed by every world religion and cult and is (at least secretly) longed for by every person.

What occurrences in daily life can provide you an opportunity to witness God's solution to this universal spiritual search? A baby's birth, a parent's death, or the death of a dream all can be springboards for sharing the hope you have in Christ. Spread the Good News!

Insights:

....

....

....

....

....

....

....

Confident in Christ

So we are always confident, even though we know that as
long as we live in these bodies we are not at home with
the Lord. For we live by believing and not by seeing.

(2 Corinthians 5:6-7)

Paul was not afraid to die because he was confident
of spending eternity with Christ. Of course, facing
the unknown may cause us anxiety and leaving loved
ones hurts deeply, but if we believe in Jesus Christ,
we can share Paul's hope and confidence of eternal
life with Him. Death is only a prelude to eternal life
with Jesus.

In Christ, we will live forever. In Christ, we have
already begun eternal life. We can confidently continue to live out our lives on earth, knowing God
will be with us. But that isn't the end. We have an
eternity to live in His presence and in His service.
Let this hope give you confidence and inspire you to
faithful service now. There is nothing to fear.

Insights:

....

....

....

....

....

....

....

....

Faith in Christ Is Enough

I am shocked that you are turning away so soon from God,
who called you to himself through the loving mercy of
Christ. You are following a different way that pretends to
be the Good News but is not the Good News at all.

(Galatians 1:6-7)

Some people were teaching "a different way" to the Gentile Christians in Galatia. These pseudo-Christian teachers believed that faith in Christ was not enough, so they were teaching that, to be saved, Gentile believers had to follow Jewish laws and customs, especially the rite of circumcision. Paul recognized, however, that this teaching was "not the Good News at all" because it undermined the truth that salvation is a gift, not a reward for certain deeds. This gift of salvation is available to all people, not just to Jews, and it is available to all who believe, not just to those who do certain things.

It is easy to slip from faith in Christ alone for salvation to a belief that faith must be supplemented by certain rituals or other actions. Genuine faith works (see Ephesians 2:8-10; James 2:14-26), but faith alone is the basis of our salvation. Beware of people who say that we need more than simple faith in Christ to be saved. When people set up additional requirements for salvation, they deny the power of Christ's death on the cross (see also Galatians 3:1-5).

Insights:

....

....

....

....

....

....

....

FAITH ALONE IS THE BASIS OF OUR SALVATION.

Love's Healing Power

For the whole law can be summed up in this one command: "Love your neighbor as yourself." But if you are always biting and devouring one another, watch out! Beware of destroying one another.

(Galatians 5:14-15)

When we lose the motivation of love, we become critical of others. We stop looking for good in them and see only their faults. Soon we lose our unity. Have you talked behind someone's back? Have you focused on others' shortcomings instead of their strengths? Remind yourself of Jesus' command to love others as you love yourself (Matthew 22:39).

When you begin to feel critical of someone, make a list of that person's positive qualities. When problems need to be addressed, confront in love rather than gossiping. If we fail to use love as our guide for action, the inevitable result is conflict among believers. This leads to disillusionment within the Christian community, which in turn can lead individuals to abandon their faith. Never lose sight of the transforming power of unselfish love and the destruction experienced when it is no longer present.

Insights:

....

....

....

....

....

....

....

....

WHEN WE LOSE THE MOTIVATION OF LOVE, WE BECOME CRITICAL OF OTHERS.

Hope for Community

For Christ himself has brought peace to us. He united Jews and Gentiles into one people when, in his own body on the cross, he broke down the wall of hostility that separated us.

(Ephesians 2:14)

There are many barriers that can divide us from other Christians: age, appearance, intelligence, political persuasion, economic status, race, theological perspective. One of the best ways to stifle Christ's love is to be friendly only with the people we like. Fortunately, Christ has knocked down the barriers and unified all believers into one family. His cross should be the focus of our unity. The Holy Spirit helps us look beyond the barriers to the unity we are called to enjoy.

Christ has destroyed the barriers people build between themselves. Because these walls have been removed, we can have real unity with people who are not like us. This is true reconciliation. Because of Christ's death, we are all one (Ephesians 2:14); our hostility against each other has been put to death (Ephesians 2:16); we can all have access to the Father by the Holy Spirit (Ephesians 2:18); we are no longer strangers or foreigners to God (Ephesians 2:19); and we are all being built into a holy temple with Christ as our chief cornerstone (Ephesians 2:20-21).

Insights:

....

....

....

....

....

....

....

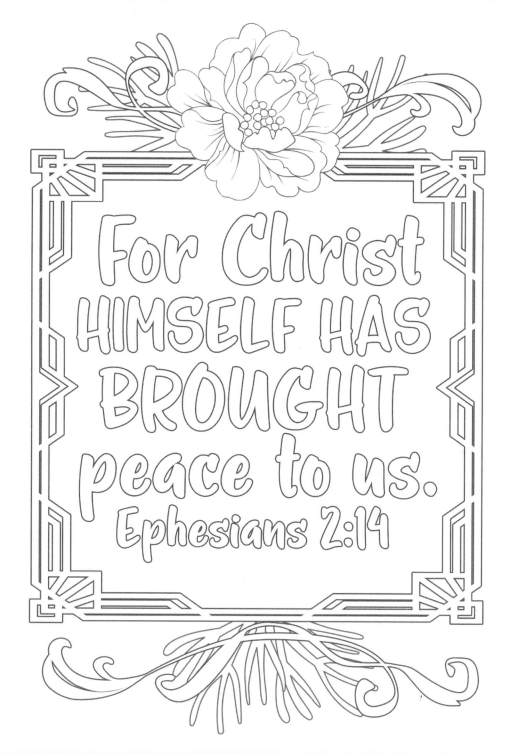

Wide, Long, High, Deep

May you have the power to understand, as all God's people should, how wide, how long, how high, and how deep his love is. May you experience the love of Christ, though it is too great to understand fully. Then you will be made complete with all the fullness of life and power that comes from God.

(Ephesians 3:18-19)

God's love is total—it reaches every corner of our experience. It is wide—it covers the breadth of our own experience, and it reaches out to the whole world. God's love is long—it continues the length of our lives. It is high—it rises to the heights of our celebration and elation. His love is deep—it reaches to the depths of our discouragement, despair, and even death.

When you feel shut out or isolated, remember you can never be lost to God's love. Wherever you've been, wherever you are, and wherever you will be, God's love is there. And such love has the power not only to rescue us from our emptiness and despair; it also fills us with life-changing power and gives us the means to offer His love to others in need. How great a gift that is!

Insights:

MAY YOU EXPERIENCE the love OF CHRIST, THOUGH IT IS too great TO UNDERSTAND fully.

EPHESIANS 3:19

Truth with Love

Instead, we will speak the truth in love, grow-
ing in every way more and more like Christ,
who is the head of his body, the church.

(Ephesians 4:15)

In describing the mature Christian, Paul says one of the marks is
the ability to "speak the truth in love." This sounds so simple, but
it seems so hard to do. Some of us are fairly good at speaking the
truth, but we forget to show love. Some of us are good at showing
love, but we don't have it in us to level with others if the truth is
painful.

The instruction here is to do both: Speak the truth, but do it in
a loving manner. Think of the trouble we would spare ourselves if
we followed this practice, especially in the church! When you have
a problem with another believer, don't go to someone else with it.
Go directly to that person and speak the truth in love. If you show
love in your approach, the listener will understand the truth you
are speaking in the best possible light. And remember that if you
fail to speak the truth, you also will have failed to demonstrate love.

Insights:

....

....

....

....

....

....

....

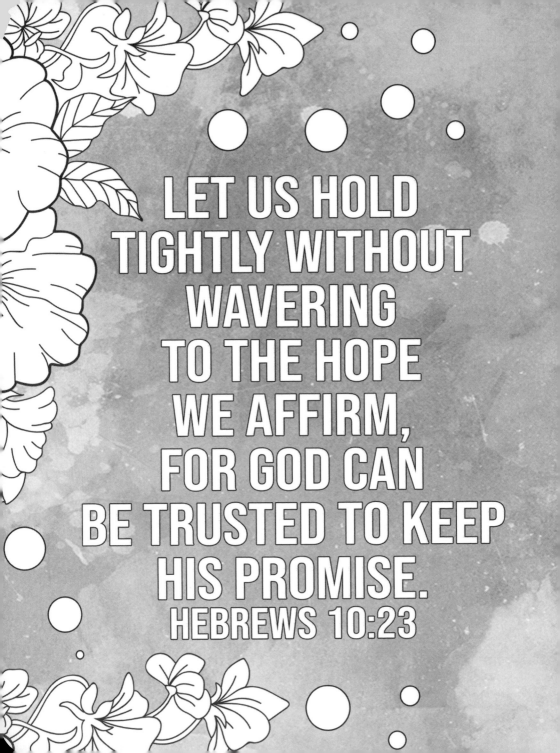

LET US HOLD TIGHTLY WITHOUT WAVERING TO THE HOPE WE AFFIRM, FOR GOD CAN BE TRUSTED TO KEEP HIS PROMISE.
HEBREWS 10:23

Free from the Past

I [Paul] focus on this one thing: Forgetting the past and
looking forward to what lies ahead, I press on to reach
the end of the race and receive the heavenly prize for
which God, through Christ Jesus, is calling us.

(Philippians 3:13-14)

Paul had reason to forget the past—he had held the
coats of those who had stoned Stephen, the first Christian martyr (Acts 7:57-58; Paul is called Saul there).
We have all done things for which we are ashamed,
and we live in the tension between what we have
been and what we want to be. Because our hope is in
Christ, however, we can let go of past guilt and look
forward to what God will help us become.

Don't dwell on your past. Instead, grow in the
knowledge of God by concentrating on your relationship with Him now. Realize that you are forgiven, and
then move on to a life of faith and obedience. Look
forward to a full, more meaningful life because of your
hope in Christ.

Insights:

....

....

....

....

....

....

....

....

Fixing Your Thoughts

And now, dear brothers and sisters, one final thing. Fix your thoughts
on what is true, and honorable, and right, and pure, and lovely, and
admirable. Think about things that are excellent and worthy of praise.

(Philippians 4:8)

What we put into our minds determines what comes out in our words
and actions. Paul tells us to program our minds with thoughts that are
true, honorable, right, pure, lovely, admirable, excellent, and worthy
of praise. There are many things we can do that will help. Pray for the
people in your life and for wisdom on how to be a blessing to them.
Read the Bible with the goal of hearing God speak, and reflect on
ways you can live out the direction He gives. Look for ways to serve
the helpless around you; look for ways to spread God's love through
both words and deeds.

Do you have problems with impure thoughts and daydreams?
Examine what you are putting into your mind through television,
Internet, books, conversations, movies, and magazines. Replace
harmful input with wholesome material. Above all, read God's Word
and pray. Ask God to help you focus your mind on what is good and
pure. It takes practice, but it can be done.

Insights:

....

....

....

....

....

....

....

....

Clothed with Love

Make allowance for each other's faults, and forgive anyone
who offends you. Remember, the Lord forgave you, so
you must forgive others. Above all, clothe yourselves with
love, which binds us all together in perfect harmony.

(Colossians 3:13-14)

Christians should live in peace. To live in peace does not mean that suddenly all differences of opinion are eliminated, but it does require that Christians work together in a loving way despite their differences. Such love is not a feeling but a decision to meet the needs of others (see 1 Corinthians 13). Clothing ourselves with love leads to peace between individuals and among the members of the body of believers. Do problems in your relationships with other Christians cause open conflicts or mutual silence? Consider what you can do to heal those relationships with love.

All the virtues Paul encourages us to develop are perfectly bound together by love. As we clothe ourselves with these virtues, the last garment we are to put on is love, which holds all the others in place. To practice any list of virtues without practicing love will lead to distortion, fragmentation, and stagnation (1 Corinthians 13:1-3).

Insights:

....

....

....

....

....

....

....

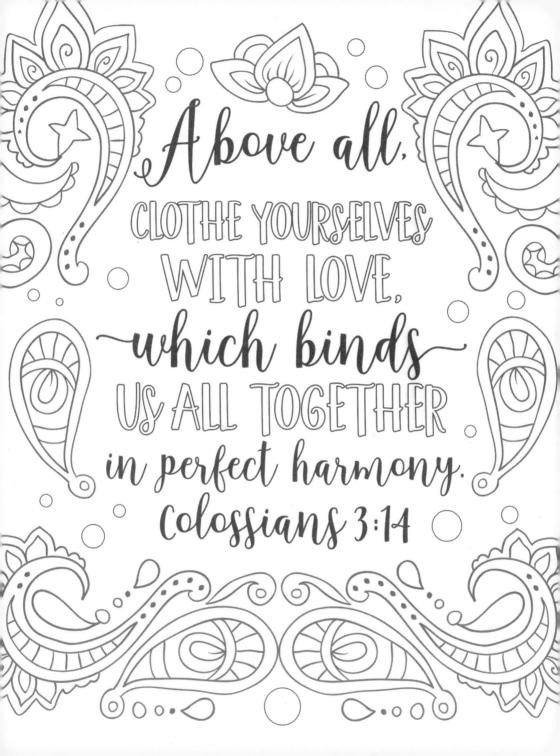

Anticipating the Benefits

And they speak of how you are looking forward to the coming of God's
Son from heaven—Jesus, whom God raised from the dead. He is the
one who has rescued us from the terrors of the coming judgment.

(1 Thessalonians 1:10)

Paul emphasized Christ's second coming throughout his letters to the Thessalonian church. Because they were being persecuted, Paul encouraged them to look forward to the deliverance that Christ would bring. A believer's hope is in the return of Jesus (Titus 2:13). Our perspective on life remains incomplete without this hope. It is essential that we keep Christ's return in mind but also that we remember that we have a calling within our broken world. Both aspects of "living in" and "looking forward" are essential to our peace as we live as Christians in this present evil age.

The "living in" is made bearable because we live for God—seeking to build His Kingdom with whatever gifts He has given us. And it is that very Kingdom to which we are "looking forward." As we live and look forward, we anticipate three great benefits of Christ's return: (1) Christ's personal presence—we look forward to being with Him. (2) Redemption from our sinful nature—we long for the end of the battle with sin and our perfection in Christ. (3) Restoration of creation—we anticipate the complete rule of grace when the image of God will be fully realized in people and the created order will be restored.

Insights:

....

....

....

....

....

....

....

....

A believer's HOPE is in the return of Jesus.

A Faithful Savior

This is a trustworthy saying: If we die with him, we will also live with him. If we endure hardship, we will reign with him. If we deny him, he will deny us. If we are unfaithful, he remains faithful, for he cannot deny who he is.

(2 Timothy 2:11-13)

This is probably an early Christian hymn. God is faithful to His children. Although we may suffer great hardships here, God promises that someday we will live eternally with Him. What will this involve? It means believers will live in Christ's Kingdom and that we will share in the administration of that Kingdom. This truth comforted Paul as he went through suffering and death. Are you facing hardships? Don't turn away from God—He promises you a wonderful future with Him. (For more information about living eternally with God, see Matthew 19:28-30; Romans 8:10-11, 17; 1 Corinthians 15:42-58; 1 Thessalonians 4:13-18; Revelation 21:1–22:21.)

Jesus is faithful. He remains even when we have endured so much that we seem to have no faith left. We may be faithless at times, but Jesus is faithful to His promise to be with us "to the end of the age" (Matthew 28:20). Refusing Christ's help will break our communication with God, but He will never turn His back on us even though we may turn our backs on Him.

Insights:

....

....

....

....

....

....

....

IF WE DIE
WITH HIM,
WE WILL ALSO
LIVE WITH HIM.
2 TIMOTHY 2:11

Hope Even in Death

Yes, and the Lord will deliver me from every evil
attack and will bring me safely into his heavenly Kingdom. All glory to God forever and ever! Amen.

(2 Timothy 4:18)

Here Paul is affirming his belief in God's protecting presence in this present life and in eternal life after death.
Paul had faced many trials and a great deal of persecution during his life, and God had protected him so he
could continue his service toward others. But Paul knew
that the end of his life was near, and he was ready for it.
Because of Paul's confidence in the promise of eternal
life, he could remain confident in God's power even as
he faced death.

Anyone facing a life-and-death struggle can be comforted knowing God will bring each believer safely
through death to His heavenly Kingdom. Entrust your
life, however long it might be, into the care of your
loving Lord. With Him, there is hope even in death.

Insights:

....

....

....

....

....

....

....

Inheritors of God's Promises

Our great desire is that you will keep on loving others as long as life lasts, in order to make certain that what you hope for will come true. Then you will not become spiritually dull and indifferent. Instead, you will follow the example of those who are going to inherit God's promises because of their faith and endurance.

(Hebrews 6:11-12)

It is easy to get discouraged, thinking God has forgotten us. But God is never unjust. He never forgets or overlooks our hard work for Him. Presently you may not be receiving rewards and acclaim, but God knows about your efforts of love and service. Let God's love for you and His intimate knowledge of your service for Him bolster you as you face disappointment and rejection here on earth.

Hope for eternal life should keep you from becoming lazy or feeling bored. Like an athlete, train hard and run well, remembering the reward that lies ahead (Philippians 3:14). Demonstrate your saving faith through action and leave a powerful legacy of love after you are gone.

Insights:

....

....

....

....

....

....

....

Boldly into God's Presence

And since we have a great High Priest who rules over God's house, let
us go right into the presence of God with sincere hearts fully trusting
him. For our guilty consciences have been sprinkled with Christ's blood
to make us clean, and our bodies have been washed with pure water.

(Hebrews 10:21-22)

How is it possible for us to "go right into the presence of God"? We
come not halfheartedly or with improper motives or pretense but with
pure, individual, and sincere worship. We can know we have "sincere
hearts" if we evaluate our thoughts and motives according to God's Word
(see Hebrews 4:12). Christians can approach God boldly, free from our
"guilty consciences" and in full assurance because of the work of Jesus
Christ. We can go to God without doubting, knowing He will hear and
answer us.

Through our relationship with Christ, our hearts and consciences are
cleansed completely, not partially or temporarily (see Hebrews 9:14).
Our clean consciences allow us to enter God's presence with boldness.
The imagery of our bodies having been "washed with pure water" actually pictures an inward cleansing. Just as baptism is an outward sign that
represents the purification Christ does inside us, so this washing speaks
of an internal cleansing from sin. Once cleansed, we can approach God.

Insights:
....
....
....
....
....
....
....

For our guilty consciences
HAVE BEEN SPRINKLED
WITH
CHRIST'S BLOOD
to make us clean.
Hebrews 10:22

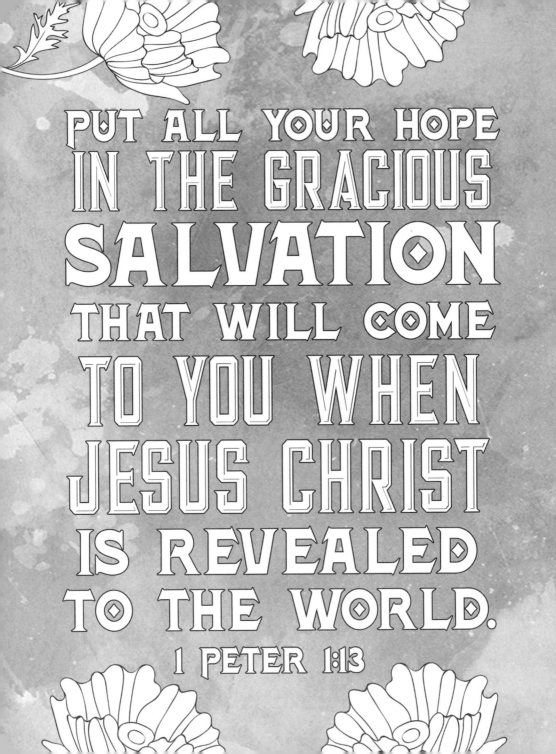

Confident Faith

Faith shows the reality of what
we hope for; it is the evidence
of things we cannot see.

(Hebrews 11:1)

Faith is, at heart, believing in God's character: He is who He says He is, and so we can trust that He will do what He says He will do. When we believe that God will fulfill His promises even though we don't see those promises materializing yet, we demonstrate true faith, not just in God's promises but in God Himself.

The definition of faith in Hebrews 11:1 begins a chapter that recounts the acts of faith of many of God's ancient people who lived before Christ came. They believed God's promise that their Messiah was coming, and they lived in light of that confident hope, even though they never saw the result—they did not live to see the Messiah come. Now He has come, and His followers have left us a record of His words and actions so that we would believe in Him (see John 20:30-31).

So now we, too, hope through faith for what we cannot yet see: we hope for eternal life, a new heaven and earth, resurrected bodies that never die, and unending sweet fellowship with God. Faith gives us confident hope that these things will happen.

Insights:

....

....

....

....

....

....

....

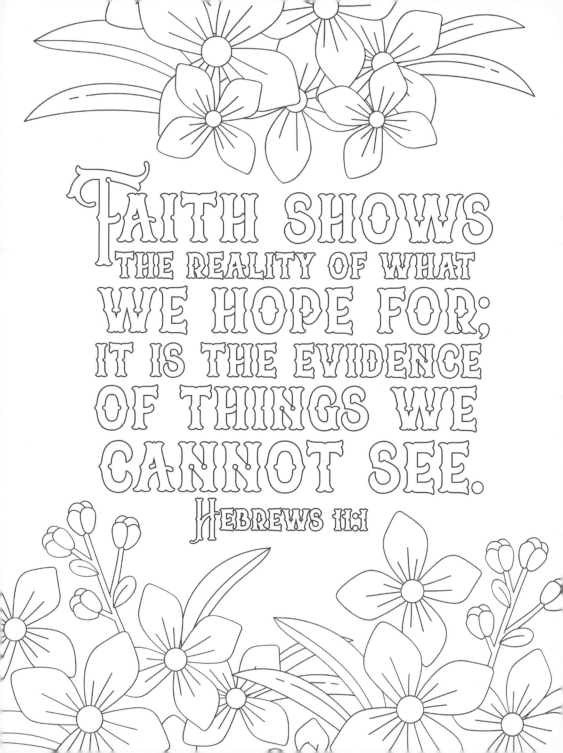

Loving Discipline

"Don't make light of the LORD's discipline, and don't give
up when he corrects you. For the LORD disciplines those he
loves, and he punishes each one he accepts as his child."

(Hebrews 12:5-6)

Discipline means "to teach and to train." Discipline sounds negative to many people because some disciplinarians aren't very loving. God, however, is the source of all love. He punishes us not because He enjoys inflicting pain but because He is deeply concerned about our growth. He knows that in order to become morally strong and good, we must learn the difference between right and wrong. His loving discipline enables us to do that.

Who loves his child more—the father who allows the child to do what will harm him or the one who corrects, trains, and even punishes the child to help him learn what is right? It's never pleasant for God to correct and discipline us, but His discipline is a sign of His deep love for us. When God corrects you, see it as proof of His love and ask Him what He is trying to teach you.

Insights:

....

....

....

....

....

....

....

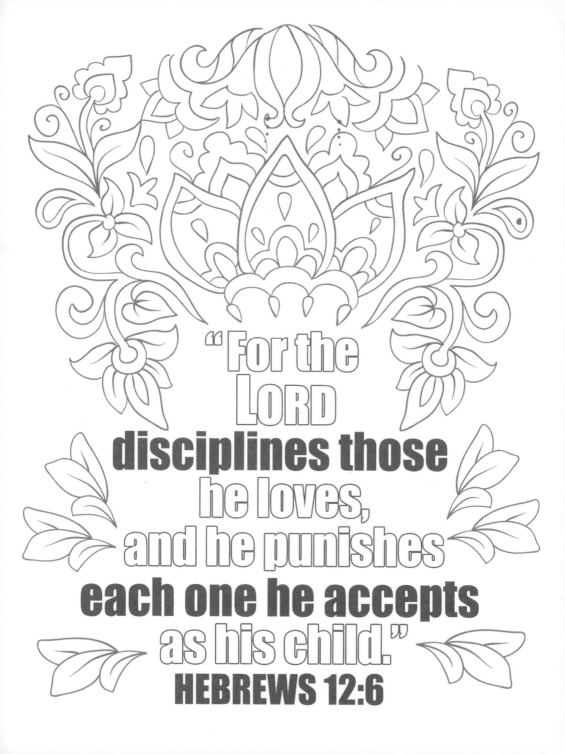

"For the LORD disciplines those he loves, and he punishes each one he accepts as his child."

HEBREWS 12:6

Tangible Love

Keep on loving each other as brothers and sisters. Don't forget to show hospitality to strangers, for some who have done this have entertained angels without realizing it! Remember those in prison, as if you were there yourself. Remember also those being mistreated, as if you felt their pain in your own bodies.

(Hebrews 13:1-3)

Real love for others produces tangible actions: (1) hospitality to strangers (Hebrews 13:2), (2) empathy for those who are in prison and those who have been mistreated (Hebrews 13:3), (3) respect for your marriage vows (Hebrews 13:4), and (4) contentment with what you have (Hebrews 13:5). Make sure your love runs deep enough to affect your hospitality, empathy, fidelity, and contentment.

Notice that loving others includes reaching out to people who, for many of us, are not in our normal line of sight, especially the strangers and prisoners. Many of us live in neighborhoods where the needy just aren't easy to see. Does that make us any less responsible to care for them? It certainly doesn't. We are called to reach out to people in need, and if our lives don't intersect much with theirs, we probably need to make some changes.

Insights:

....

....

....

....

....

....

....

Results of Faith

My dear brothers and sisters, how can you claim to have faith in our
glorious Lord Jesus Christ if you favor some people over others? . . .
What good is it, dear brothers and sisters, if you say you have faith but
don't show it by your actions? Can that kind of faith save anyone?

(James 2:1, 14)

Right actions are the natural by-products of true faith. A genuine Christian
will have a changed life (James 2:18). Even though, as Paul says, "we are
made right with God through faith and not by obeying the law" (Romans
3:28), nevertheless true faith always results in good deeds.

On the other hand, so-called faith without good deeds doesn't do
anybody any good—it is useless (James 2:14-17). In fact, even demons
"believe" in the sense that they know who Jesus is, but their existence is in
no way bent toward obeying Him (James 2:19). Mere intellectual assent is
quite distinct from true faith. If we really believe in Jesus and trust in God,
we will do as He says. True faith involves willing obedience to God.

We must serve God and others with compassion, speak lovingly and
truthfully, live in obedience to God's commands, and love one another.
Believers ought to be examples of heaven on earth, drawing people to
Christ through love for God and each other. If we truly believe God's
Word, we will live it day by day.

Insights:

....

....

....

....

....

....

....

RIGHT ACTIONS
are the natural
BY-PRODUCTS
of true faith.

Loving without Prejudice

Yes indeed, it is good when you obey the royal law as
found in the Scriptures: "Love your neighbor as yourself." But if you favor some people over others, you are
committing a sin. You are guilty of breaking the law.

(James 2:8-9)

Christians must obey the law of love, which supersedes both
religious and civil laws. How easy it is to excuse our indiffer-
ence to others merely because we have no legal obligation to
help them and even can justify harming them if our actions
are technically legal! But Jesus does not leave loopholes in the
law of love. Whenever love demands it, we are to go beyond
human legal requirements and imitate the God of love.

We must treat all people as we want to be treated. There
is no place for prejudice or partiality when it comes to love.
We should not ignore the wealthy because that would be
withholding our love. But we must not favor the rich for
what they can do for us while ignoring the poor who can
offer seemingly little in return. Love demands that we treat all
people the same, just as God does.

Insights:

....

....

....

....

....

....

....

....

Reward for Trusting Him

You love him even though you have never seen him.
Though you do not see him now, you trust him; and you
rejoice with a glorious, inexpressible joy. The reward for
trusting him will be the salvation of your souls.

(1 Peter 1:8-9)

Peter wrote to Christians who had never seen Jesus personally but even so had believed the message about Jesus and had put their faith in Him for salvation. They had formed a personal relationship with Christ Himself, their Savior whom they had never met in the flesh. They loved Him, devoted their lives to Him even through all kinds of trials and difficulties (1 Peter 1:6-7), and had great joy. They had learned to live by faith in Christ. As a result, they were sure of the reward they would have: salvation for their souls.

We are in the same position as those long-ago Christians who believed without having met Jesus personally. We, too, have received from Jesus' apostles a report of His words and deeds, especially His death for our sin and His resurrection to eternal life. We, too, have the opportunity to trust Him without having seen Him. As we do, we, too, can experience "glorious, inexpressible joy" in Him and have the same confidence that we, too, will have salvation for our souls. How blessed are those who are saved by the Lord!

Insights:

....
....
....
....
....
....
....
....

The reward FOR TRUSTING him will be THE SALVATION of your souls.
1 PETER 1:9

Sharing Our Hope

But even if you suffer for doing what is right, God will reward you for it. So don't worry or be afraid of their threats. Instead, you must worship Christ as Lord of your life. And if someone asks about your hope as a believer, always be ready to explain it.

(1 Peter 3:14-15)

Some Christians believe faith is a personal matter that should be kept to oneself. It is true we shouldn't be offensive or obnoxious in sharing our faith, but we should always be ready to give an answer, gently and respectfully, when asked about our faith, our lifestyle, or our Christian perspective.

Can others see your hope in Christ? Are you prepared to tell them what Christ has done in your life? You don't have to be a theologian to do this. Just talk about how Christ has touched your life and the hope you have because of Him. The personal story of how your life has been changed will be far more powerful than any theological argument you could make.

Insights:

....

....

....

....

....

....

....

....

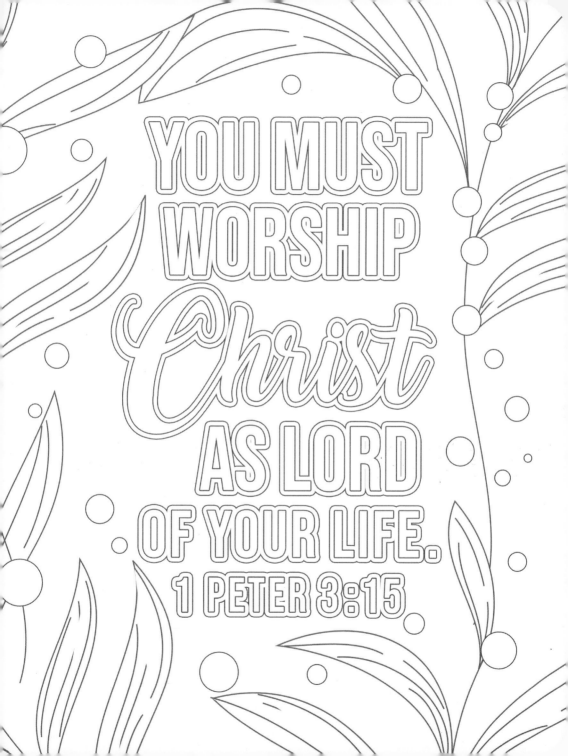

Safe in God's Hands

So humble yourselves under the mighty power of God,
and at the right time he will lift you up in honor. Give all
your worries and cares to God, for he cares about you.

(1 Peter 5:6-7)

Carrying your worries, stresses, and daily struggles
by yourself shows you have not trusted God fully
with your life. It takes humility, however, to recognize that God cares, to admit your need, and to let
others in God's family help you. When you honor
God by humbling yourself before Him, He in turn
will lift you up.

Sometimes we think that the struggles caused by
our own sin and foolishness are not God's concern.
But when we turn to God in repentance, He will
bear the weight even of those struggles. Letting God
have your anxieties calls for action, not passivity.
Don't submit to circumstances; instead, submit to
the Lord, who controls circumstances.

Insights:

....

....

....

....

....

....

....

....

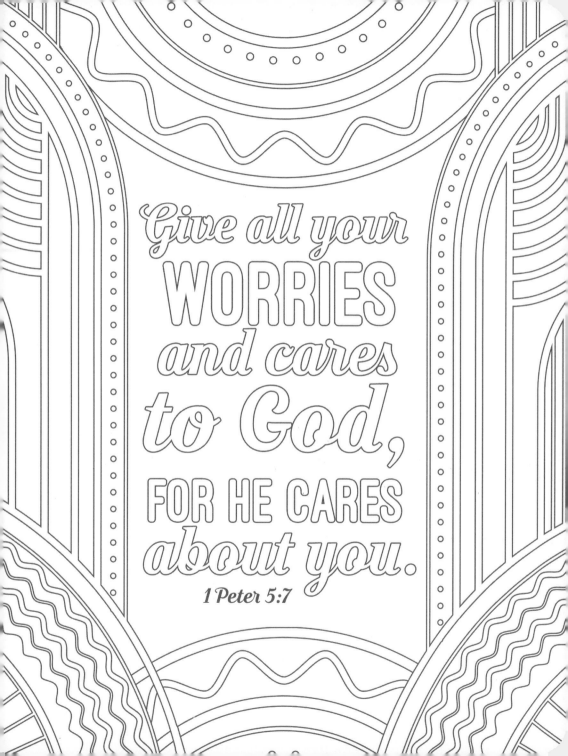

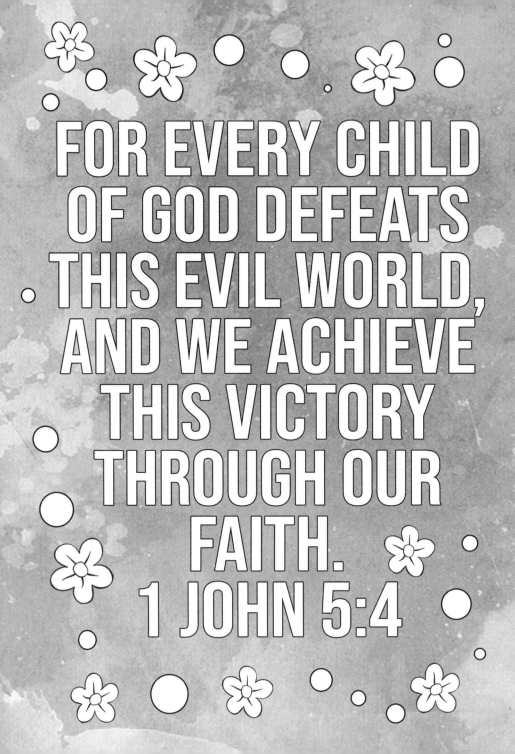

Loving Like God

Dear friends, let us continue to love one another,
for love comes from God. Anyone who loves is a
child of God and knows God. But anyone who does
not love does not know God, for God is love.

(1 John 4:7-8)

John says, "God is love," not "Love is God." Our world, with its shallow and selfish view of love, has turned these words around and contaminated our understanding of love. The world thinks that love is what makes a person feel good and that it is all right to sacrifice moral principles and others' rights in order to obtain such "love." But that isn't real love; it is the exact opposite—selfishness. And God is not that kind of "love."

Real love is like God, who is holy, just, and perfect. If we truly know God, we will love as He does. God loves us all, even when we are unlovely to Him; we should do the same for others. God reaches out to bring us help and healing; we should do the same for others. God forgives us even when we don't deserve it; we should do the same for others. If we fail to love unselfishly, we prove that we don't know God at all, because He is love.

Insights:

_____

_____

_____

_____

_____

_____

_____

Awakening Our Love

> "I have this complaint against you [the church in Ephesus]. You don't love me or each other as you did at first! Look how far you have fallen! Turn back to me and do the works you did at first. If you don't repent, I will come and remove your lampstand from its place among the churches."
>
> *(Revelation 2:4-5)*

Paul had once commended the church at Ephesus for its love for God and others (Ephesians 1:15), but many of the church founders had died, and many of the second-generation believers had lost their zeal for God. They were a busy church—the members did much to benefit themselves and the community—but they were acting out of the wrong motives. Work for God must be motivated by love for God, or it will not last.

Just as when a man and woman fall in love, so also new believers rejoice at their newfound forgiveness. But when we lose sight of the seriousness of sin, we begin to lose the thrill of our forgiveness (see 2 Peter 1:9). In the first steps of your Christian life, you may have had enthusiasm without knowledge. Do you now have knowledge without enthusiasm? Both are necessary if we are to keep love for God intense and untarnished (see Hebrews 10:32, 35). Do you love God with the same fervor as when you were a new Christian?

Insights:

....

....

....

....

....

....

....

....

Work for God MUST BE MOTIVATED BY LOVE FOR God, or it will not last.

Everything New

And the one sitting on the throne said,
"Look, I am making everything new!" And
then he said to me, "Write this down, for
what I tell you is trustworthy and true."

(Revelation 21:5)

God is the Creator. The Bible begins with the
majestic story of His creating the universe, and it
concludes with His creating a new heaven and a
new earth. This is a tremendous hope and encour-
agement for the believer. When we are with God,
with our sins forgiven and our future secure, we
will be like Christ. We will be made perfect like
Him.

Revelation is, above all, a book of hope. It
shows that no matter what happens on earth, God
is in control. It promises that evil will not last forever. And it depicts the wonderful reward waiting
for all those who believe in Jesus Christ as Savior
and Lord.

Insights:

....

....

....

....

....

....

....

....

A Future Hope

He who is the faithful witness to all these things says, "Yes,
I am coming soon!" Amen! Come, Lord Jesus! May the
grace of the Lord Jesus be with God's holy people.

(Revelation 22:20-21)

Revelation closes human history as Genesis opened it—in paradise. But there is one distinct difference in Revelation—evil is gone forever. Genesis describes Adam and Eve walking and talking with God; Revelation describes people worshiping God face-to-face. Genesis describes a garden with an evil serpent; Revelation describes a perfect city with no evil. The Garden of Eden was destroyed by sin, but paradise is re-created in the new Jerusalem.

The book of Revelation ends with an urgent plea: "Come, Lord Jesus!" In a world of problems, persecution, evil, and immorality, Christ calls us to endure in our faith. Our efforts to better our world are important, but their results cannot compare with the transformation Jesus will bring about when He returns. He alone controls human history, forgives sin, and will re-create the earth and bring lasting peace.

Insights:

....

....

....

....

....

....

....

Inspire *The Bible for Coloring & Creative Journaling*

Original Edition

Hardcover LeatherLike
978-1-4964-1374-1

Large Print LeatherLike
978-1-4964-1986-6

Praise Edition

LeatherLike
978-1-4964-2984-1

Large Print HC
LeatherLike
978-1-4964-3346-6

Prayer Edition

LeatherLike
978-1-4964-2409-9

Giant Print LeatherLike
978-1-4964-5497-3

Girls Edition

Softcover
978-1-4964-2661-1

HC LeatherLike
978-1-4964-2665-9

LeatherLike
978-1-4964-5495-9

Catholic Bible

HC LeatherLike
978-1-4964-3657-3

Large Print
LeatherLike
978-1-4964-4683-1

LeatherLike
978-1-4964-5496-6

Coloring-Book Style

Inspire: Psalms
978-1-4964-1987-3

Inspire: Proverbs
978-1-4964-2664-2

Inspire: Matthew & Mark
978-1-4964-5498-0

Inspire: Luke & John
978-1-4964-5499-7

Inspire: Acts & Romans
978-1-4964-5500-0

Inspire: 1 Cor—2 Thes
978-1-4964-5501-7

Inspire: 1 Tim—Rev
978-1-4964-5502-4